HOW DOES
JESUS
FULFILL THE
OLD TESTAMENT?

MICHAEL J. VLACH

Theological
STUDIES PRESS

Vlach, Michael, 1966 –
How Does Jesus Fulfill the Old Testament? / Michael J. Vlach

ISBN: 978-0-9798539-7-5

Printed in the United States of America

CONTENTS

PREFACE

This book offers an introduction to how Jesus fulfills the Old Testament. Its primary aim is to positively present how Jesus fulfills God's purposes as revealed in the Hebrew Scriptures. A secondary goal is to address a concern of mine that the concept of "fulfillment in Jesus" is often misunderstood or misapplied in ways that diminish the integrity of God's promises and wrongly alters the Bible's storyline.

One common misunderstanding is the tendency to interpret fulfillment in Jesus as a mystical or symbolic transformation, where Old Testament realities vanish or are dissolved into the person of Christ, losing their historical significance. This view, referred to as *metaphysical personalism*, holds that Old Testament promises are absorbed or transformed into Christ, with little regard for their concrete fulfillment in history.

While Christ is the central focus of God's plans, His role must be understood rightly. I will argue against metaphysical personalism and show that Jesus fulfills God's promises by bringing them to completion in a deeper, more profound, and literal way—without diminishing their original meaning or intent.

I will demonstrate that Jesus is the active means by which the Old Testament is fulfilled—in all its details and with all the parties to whom promises were made. This includes His fulfillment of messianic prophecies, messianic roles, the rites and festivals of the Mosaic Covenant, Israel's hope for a permanent exodus, and all eschatological promises. In passages like Matthew 5:17–18, Jesus affirms that He has come not to abolish the Law or the Prophets, but to fulfill them—ensuring that everything foretold in the Old Testament will be accomplished.

1

Acts 3:20–21 further attests to this, showing that Jesus is the One who will bring about the "restoration of all things" that the prophets foretold.

I aim to offer a clearer understanding of how Jesus fulfills these Old Testament promises—not by dissolving them, but by completing them in a way that reveals their fullest meaning. This positive understanding of fulfillment is central to the argument I will develop here, and I will focus on several key examples to illustrate what fulfillment in Jesus really means.

The topic of Jesus' fulfillment of the Old Testament is vast and complex. And the reader should note this book is intentionally brief. It is not an exhaustive reference work. My goal is to provide a clear and accessible introduction, focusing on key issues and examples that most effectively highlight the relationship between Jesus and Old Testament expectations. I do not attempt to cover every instance of fulfillment, but rather select several key examples that demonstrate the broader patterns at work. Through these examples, I hope to encourage a deeper appreciation for the unity of Scripture and a fuller understanding of how Jesus is the fulfillment of all God's promises, as seen in both the Old and New Testaments.

CHAPTER ONE

THE DEBATE OVER JESUS AND OLD TESTAMENT FULFILLMENT

If you were to ask a group of one hundred Christians if Jesus fulfills the Old Testament they all probably would raise their hands to affirm this. In fact, I cannot think of any true Christ-follower who would argue otherwise. But if you were to ask, "How does Jesus fulfill the Old Testament specifically?" you probably would get some pauses and quizzical looks, perhaps some hesitant and disjointed answers. That Jesus fulfills the Old Testament is something we affirm, though not many can explain what this means.

Most Christians understand Jesus literally accomplished certain prophecies such as the Messiah being born in Bethlehem (Matt. 2:5–6/Micah 5:2) and Jesus suffering for our sins (Luke 22:37/Isaiah 53:12). But some also believe "fulfillment in Jesus" means certain Old Testament promises and predictions somehow vanish, absorb, dissolve, or transform into Jesus. This often occurs with Old Testament prophecies about Israel, nations, physical blessings, an earthly kingdom, land, temple, Jerusalem, and other tangible realities.

In a theology class, a few years ago, I argued that Jesus will fulfill certain Old Testament land and physical promises for Israel based on Old Testament texts like Deuteronomy 30:1–10; Leviticus 26:40–45; Jeremiah 30–33 and others. By "fulfill" I meant happen as stated. Just as Israel's past dispersions and captivities involved land and material consequences for the nation, so, too, Israel's future salvation and restoration would involve matters like land and agricultural prosperity. One student, though, objected, saying, "But aren't all the promises of God fulfilled in Jesus?" He then appealed to 2 Corinthians 1:20a which states, " For as many as are the promises of God, in Him [Jesus] they are yes." He thought there would be no literal completion of land and physical promises for Israel since Jesus already "fulfilled" all of God's promises. By "fulfill" he meant absorb or dissolve. Since Jesus was the fulfillment of Israel, the details of Old Testament prophecies merged into Him in such a way that literal accomplishment of the details of these promises was no longer necessary. Why look for a literal fulfillment of Old Testament promises for Israel, when they were all "fulfilled" with Jesus, the true Israelite, at His first coming? It struck me that he and I were operating from differing assumptions of what "fulfillment in Jesus" actually meant.

On another occasion someone said, "I no longer believe in a future for national Israel like you do because Jesus is the true Israel and He fulfills the promises made to Israel." For this person too, the details of Old Testament prophecies for Israel were subsumed into Jesus in such a way that a literal accomplishment of prophetic details concerning Israel vanished into Christ. Again, varying beliefs of what fulfillment in Jesus means were in play.

This kind of thinking appears frequently. One can see it on social media discussions about theology. And it also shows up extensively in academic books and articles. A common perception exists that Jesus transforms or dissolves Old Testament promises into himself so that a literal fulfillment of their details will not happen. But is this accurate?

The confusion concerning what it means for Jesus to fulfill the Old Testament is the reason for this book. Since God's purposes in Jesus are so important and God ties His character to accomplishing what He has promised, we must get this issue right. As I study Jesus and fulfillment in the Bible, I do not see this idea of Jesus as the dissolver or transformer of Old Testament expectations. As Robert Saucy rightly states, "The truth that all the promises are fulfilled in Christ does not, as some say, dissolve their meaning into the person of Christ."[1] Fulfillment in Jesus does not mean absorb, transform, or vanish. What Jesus does concerning the Old Testament is much better and grander than that.

Methodology

How does one go about understanding Old Testament fulfillment in Jesus? Instead of trusting assumptions of what fulfillment in Jesus means, we need to inductively look at how the Bible presents fulfillment of the Old Testament in Jesus. This means looking at the biblical data and drawing the right implications. This includes:

1.   Understanding the Old Testament well—its key themes, persons, events, covenants, etc.

2.   Looking at key "fulfillment" terms, formulas, and terminology in the New Testament—especially *pleroō*.

---

1   Robert L. Saucy, *The Case for Progressive Dispensationalism: The Interface Between Dispensational & Non-Dispensational Theology* (Grand Rapids: Zondervan, 1993), 32.

3.   Studying all texts that connect Jesus with the Old Testament, directly and indirectly.

4.   Drawing correct implications and significances from the meaning of texts that connect Jesus and the Old Testament.

In this work, we will argue that Jesus is the *means* for the accomplishment of the Old Testament in all its details. Everything stated and predicted in the Old Testament will happen because of and through Jesus. Jesus does not mystically dissolve Old Testament prophecies and promises into himself. Instead, He takes it upon himself to bring about the accomplishment of all God's plans. As we will show, the fulfillment of the Old Testament through Jesus occurs in six main ways:

1.   *Jesus Accomplishes the Specific Details of Messianic Prophecies*

2.   *Jesus Completes Messianic Hope Expectations*

3.   *Jesus Realizes Israel's Hope of Exodus from Exile (Correspondence + Messianic Hope)*

4.   *Jesus Culminates Patterns that began with David*

5.   *Jesus Is the Substance of Mosaic Covenant Ceremonies and Feasts*

6.   *Jesus Guarantees the Future Fulfillment of Old Testament Prophecies that Have Not Occurred Yet*

How Jesus Relates to the Categories of Fulfillment

With this perspective, Jesus is at the center of God's purposes, and Jesus works to accomplish everything in the Old Testament. Jesus does not absorb or subsume the Old Testament promises in some mystical way. He does not make Old Testament prophecies, promises, and covenants vanish or dissolve into himself. He actively works to bring all of God's purposes to completion in all of their dimensions. Not only is this position accurate, but it is also more honoring to God and Jesus than is the alternative view.

We must add an important note before going forward. As we examine the biblical evidence concerning Jesus and fulfillment, we must grasp that God's plans are intricate and multifaceted. This complexity is reflected in how Jesus fulfills the Old Testament, which encompasses strategic events; themes; individuals; and multi-dimensional promises, covenants, and prophecies made with several parties—each contributing to a grand narrative. If God's purposes are complex and multi-faceted, so too will fulfillment in Jesus be. Jesus is deeply connected to all these elements, and His fulfilling these areas is uniquely suited to each one. Thus, fulfillment can have a nuanced meaning based on the category being fulfilled.

For instance, the way Jesus fulfills specific messianic prophecies looks a little different from how He fulfills the feasts of Israel. Also, the fulfillment of messianic roles like Last Adam and Davidic King is not the same as the fulfillment of geo-political battles between nations as seen in texts like Daniel 11. In addition, since there are two comings of Jesus, some fulfillments occur with Jesus' first advent, while other fulfillments happen with Jesus' second coming. So when we say Jesus is the fulfillment of Israel's exodus from exile, this does not mean that event has happened yet, but it will at Jesus' second coming. These distinctions are crucial for understanding the multifaceted nature of Christ's fulfillment of the Old Testament. Jesus is the means for all of these. And we can say they are "literally fulfilled." But since we are dealing with differing categories, what fulfillment looks like can vary. The material in the chart below will be discussed in more detail as we proceed, but it gives an overview of Jesus and the categories of fulfillment:

Old Testament Theme	Fulfillment in Jesus
Patterns in History	Jesus → Completes/ends Israel's exile with a New Exodus
Biblical Covenants	Jesus → Brings the realization of all details of all covenants
Promises	Jesus → Brings all promises to completion in all their details
Key Persons	Jesus → Finishes the roles of Last Adam, ultimate Davidic King, and others
Messianic Prophecies	Jesus → Accomplishes all the details of prophecies concerning the Messiah
Messianic Hope Expectations	Jesus → Brings to pass all messianic hope expectations for a Savior, Curse-Remover, Warrior, Last Adam, Davidic King, etc.
Mosaic Feasts and Ceremonies	Jesus → Embodies the substance of what the Mosaic feasts and ceremonies represented
Other Prophecies	Jesus → Works for and guarantees the completion of all Old Testament prophecies in all their details

Jesus is the means through which the entire Old Testament is fulfilled, though the manner of fulfillment can vary based on the specific entity or event being addressed. So when Paul declares in 2 Corinthians 1:20 that all the promises of God are "Yes in Him" [Jesus], we must understand that this "Yes" is not one-dimensional, but varies depending on the specific promise or event being fulfilled. As Craig Blaising observes, the phrase "in Him" can be understood as meaning "through Him," emphasizing Jesus as the channel through which God's promises are realized:

> Actually, "in Him" is a thick concept in Scripture that includes "through Him." It includes multiple aspects of the relationship of Christ to the redeemed creation.[2]

---

2   Craig A. Blaising, "A Critique of Gentry and Wellum's, *Kingdom Through Covenant*: A Hermeneutical-Theological Response," *Master's Seminary Journal* 26.1 (Spring 2015): 124.

CHAPTER TWO

DOES JESUS MAKE OLD TESTAMENT PROMISES VANISH?

The majority of this book is a positive presentation of what fulfillment in Jesus means. But first, we want to discuss an erroneous view. This is the perspective that major Old Testament promises, prophecies, and covenants vanish, dissolve, transform, or absorb into Jesus in such a way that the details of these will not be accomplished. The method for doing this will often sound very good. Some will appeal to "Christocentric hermeneutics." Others will say they are interpreting the Old Testament promises "through the lens of Christ." Others will claim that there is an "apostolic hermeneutic" that changes the meaning of Old Testament realities. Some will claim "New Testament priority" or something else. Our purposes here do not allow for a full examination and critique of these approaches. But one should be aware that many will use Jesus and the New Testament as a reason for spiritualizing or transforming Old Testament promises. But this approach does not pass biblical scrutiny. Understanding Jesus and fulfillment can be found through consistent grammatical-historical interpretation that accounts for the context of all Bible passages. This includes the proper interpretation for the meaning of these passages and the significances and applications that stem from the proper meaning.

A formal title for the view that Jesus transforms or makes Old Testament prophecies vanish is metaphysical personalism. With metaphysical personalism details of Old Testament prophecies and promises allegedly morph, dissolve, or vanish into the person of Jesus in some mystical way.[3] For example, Kim Riddlebarger, a representative of Amillennialism, argues against literal fulfillment of Old Testament physical promises to the nation Israel because Christ is the "true Israel." He says:

> The New Testament writers claimed that Jesus was the true Israel of God and the fulfillment of Old Testament prophecies. So what remains of the dispensationalists' case that these prophecies will yet be fulfilled in a future millennium? They vanish in Jesus Christ, who has fulfilled them.[4]

Note Riddlebarger's use of "vanish" concerning "Old Testament prophecies." Old Testament predictions concerning an earthly kingdom allegedly "vanish in Jesus Christ, who has fulfilled them." This is metaphysical personalism because the content of Old Testament prophecies vanish mystically into the person of Christ.

---

3   The reference to "metaphysical Personalism" was found in Blaising's response to Progressive Covenantalism's use of the person of Christ: "KTC [*Kingdom Through Covenant*], at times, reads the Person of Christ as Himself the mystical consummation of the whole narrative. He personally is the fulfillment of Israel, the land, the nation, the church, the creation. The result is a vague mysticism that looks somewhat like a variant of metaphysical Personalism." Craig A. Blaising, "A Critique of Gentry and Wellum's, *Kingdom Through Covenant*: A Hermeneutical-Theological Response," *The Master's Seminary Journal* 26.1 (Spring 2015): 124.

4   Kim Riddlebarger, *A Case for Amillennialism: Understanding the End Times* (Grand Rapids: Baker, 2003), 70.

Also adopting a metaphysical personalism approach, covenant theologian, Mark Karlberg, believes Old Testament prophecies about national Israel's kingdom will be "dissolved":

> In that day the typological phenomenon of the ancient Israelite theocracy would be dissolved into the antitypical reality of the Church as the New Israel.[5]

In his discussion of why Old Testament prophecies concerning an earthly kingdom will not occur literally, Robert Strimple claims that because of Jesus "fulfillment may transcend the terms in which a promise is presented."[6]

In his book, *Gospel and Kingdom*, Graeme Goldsworthy asserts that the Old Testament will not be fulfilled literally because of Jesus:

> For the New Testament the interpretation of the Old Testament is not "literal" but "Christological". That is to say that the coming of the Christ transforms all the Kingdom terms of the Old Testament into gospel reality.[7]

This quote reveals several noteworthy points. First, for Goldsworthy, a literal-contextual fulfillment of the Old Testament will not occur. Second, the reason for this alleged non-literal fulfillment of the Old Testament is Jesus. He claims Jesus

5   Mark W. Karlberg, "The Significance of Israel in Biblical Typology," in *Journal of the Evangelical Theological Society* 31.3 (1988): 267.

6   Robert B. Strimple, "Amillennialism," in *Three Views on the Millennium and Beyond*, ed. Darrell L. Bock (Grand Rapids: Zondervan, 1999), 99.

7   Graeme Goldsworthy, *Gospel and Kingdom: A Christian Interpretation of the Old Testament* (Carlisle: Paternoster, 1994), 88.

"transforms" all kingdom terms in the Old Testament into gospel reality. Third, because of Jesus, the Bible interpreter should abandon "literal" interpretation for "Christological" interpretation. So Jesus supposedly changes and transforms the message and prophecies of the Old Testament.

Gary Burge also is a major proponent of a mystical fulfillment in Jesus approach. He argues against a literal fulfillment of Old Testament land promises to Israel because of the person of Jesus. He says: *"Divine space is now no longer located in a place but in a person."*[8] Note that Burge claims, "divine space," regarding a geographical locale can have its significance transcended in Jesus. Also, concerning John 15, Burge says, "In a word, *Jesus spiritualizes the land."*[9]

In his article, "4 Ways Jesus Fulfills Every Old Testament Promise," Jason DeRouchie posits that "Christ Transforms Some Old Testament Promises."[10] To support this he says:

> At times, Jesus transforms or develops the makeup and audience of an Old Testament promise. These promises relate most directly to shadows that clarify and point to a greater substance in Christ—that is, to Old Testament patterns or types that find their climax or antitype in Jesus.[11]

---

8   Gary M. Burge, *Jesus and the Land: The New Testament Challenge to "Holy Land" Theology* (Grand Rapids: Baker, 2010), 52. Emphases in original.

9   Ibid., 56. Emphases in original.

10   Jason DeRouchie, "4 Ways Jesus Fulfills Every Old Testament Promise," https://jasonderouchie.com/4-ways-jesus-fulfills-every-old-testament-promise/ February 18, 2024 (accessed January 2, 2025). Emphases in original.

11   Ibid.

The main example he offers concerns the land promises to Israel in the Old Testament. As he notes above, promises about Israel's land relate "directly to shadows" that "point to a greater substance in Christ." For DeRouchie, Romans 4:13 is support for his view:

> In the new covenant, Christ transforms the type into the antitype by fulfilling the original land promise in himself and by extending it to the whole world through his people. In Paul's words, God promised "Abraham and his offspring that he would be heir of the *world*" (Rom. 4:13); at the consummation the new earth will fully realize the antitype. By extending the promised land to lands, Jesus transforms Israel's "everlasting possession" (Gen. 17:8; 48:4), realizing what God had already foretold to the patriarchs.[12]

With this author's perspective, specific land promises to Israel filter through Jesus in a way that removes their particular fulfillment with Israel. So a transforming or dissolving of Israel's land promises in Jesus occurs. The result, though, is not a total spiritualizing of the land, since the land promise comes out the other side by "extending it to the whole world." But if we are understanding him correctly, there will be no literal fulfillment of land promises to Israel because they are transformed through Jesus and then extend to the whole earth for all peoples.

---

12   Ibid.

Responses to
Metaphysical Personalism

We do not agree with the metaphysical personalism view of fulfillment in Jesus for several reasons. First, no biblical data exists for the theory that Jesus dissolves, transforms or makes Old Testament promises vanish in Him. As we look at the thirty occasions where the main "fulfillment" term in the New Testament is used concerning Jesus and the Old Testament— *pleroō*—none mean vanish, transform, or dissolve. Also, as we have examined the approximately three-hundred fifty quotations of the Old Testament in the New Testament we do not see promises metaphysically vanishing into Jesus.

And there certainly is no pattern of this type of mystical fulfillment in the Bible. The texts used to support the metaphysical personalism perspective do not actually support this view. As we study "fulfill" language in Scripture we have yet to see an example where the dissolving, transforming, or vanishing of Old Testament prophecies and promises occurs.

Second, as we will see in the upcoming chapters, Jesus' role is to accomplish God's purposes in all their dimensions as stated in the Old Testament, not dissolve or transform them. God cannot lie and He does not deceive. An ethical component exists when a promise-maker makes a promise to an audience. Because God is a faithful covenant-keeping God, He will complete the content of the promises as stated to the original audience. Not doing so would mean breaking His promise.

Third, we also think that those who argue that Jesus transforms and dissolves promises into himself have adopted an over-spiritualized worldview or perspective on God's purposes. God's plans involve the earth. They involve nations. They include Israel. God's plans involve land, and they include physical blessings. Why must these areas be dissolved into Jesus when they are important parts of God's historical purposes? The Bible does not teach the transforming of these tangible entities into Jesus; it affirms the importance of these matters. Ironically, the metaphysical personalism approach believes it is giving glory to Christ, but in reality it detracts from His glory by blurring how Jesus interacts with creation. As Blaising explains:

> While this may seem to exalt the Person of Christ, it actually diminishes Him, because it threatens the integrity of the communion of attributes that gives Him a distinguishable identity within and among His creatures while at the same time affirming His divine transcendence and immanence. It diminishes His Person because it deprives Him of the rich, thick inheritance that Scripture predicts for Him, an inheritance that retains the integrity of its created reality as the earth and the heavens, land and lands, people and peoples as individuals and as nations, including Israel and all the Gentiles, all worshipful of Him and in service to Him, not mystically dissolved into the reality of His person.[13]

Jesus as a person is distinct from other persons, things, and events. While Jesus is central and most important, other persons, things, and events matter because they are related to God's purposes. And Jesus works to complete all of God's plans in all of their details because the details matter. Metaphysical personalism is more akin to the eschatology of eastern religions like Hinduism or Buddhism, where the goal is the mystical merging of all things into the Absolute. But the Christian worldview is not like that.

---

13 Blaising, "A Critique of Gentry and Wellum's, *Kingdom Through Covenant*: A Hermeneutical-Theological Response," 125.

Finally, and our focus going forward, the main reason to reject metaphysical personalism is because of what the Bible positively says about fulfillment in Jesus. When we look at what fulfillment in Jesus means we see various dimensions of fulfillment, but metaphysical personalism is not one of them.

CHAPTER THREE

JESUS AS MEANS OF OLD TESTAMENT FULFILLMENT: KEY TEXTS

We now move to a positive presentation concerning how Jesus fulfills the Old Testament. This comes in two stages. First, with this chapter, we examine key texts that directly address the issue of Jesus and Old Testament fulfillment—Matthew 5:17-18; and Romans 15:8–9. Matthew 5:17–18 is particularly significant since Jesus himself states His relationship to the fulfillment of the Old Testament Scriptures. With Romans 15:8–9, Paul explains Jesus' Servant-role in fulfilling God's promises to Israel and Gentiles. We also comment on Matthew 3:15 and what it means for Jesus to fulfill all righteousness. In short, these passages show that Jesus is God's intended means for the accomplishment of all God's purposes.

Then the chapters after this will look more specifically at the specific ways Jesus fulfills Old Testament promises, prophecies, and covenants. They reveal how Jesus relates to messianic prophecies; messianic hope expectations; patterns between Jesus, Israel, and David; the Mosaic Covenant and its ceremonies; and prophecies that still await future fulfillment.

Matthew 5:17–18:
Jesus Guarantees Everything in the Old Testament Will Be Fulfilled

As Jesus delivered His Sermon on the Mount (Matthew 5–7) He knew some thought He was discarding the Hebrew Scriptures. Jesus responded to this erroneous charge in Matthew 5:17–18:

> "Do not think that I came to abolish the Law or the Prophets;
> I did not come to abolish but to fulfill. For truly I say to you,
> until heaven and earth pass away, not the smallest letter or
> stroke shall pass from the Law until all is accomplished."

The significance of this statement for Jesus' relationship to the Old Testament is great. But before diving into the details of this text we want to state upfront what we think Jesus' main point is. *With Matthew 5:17–18, Jesus asserts that everything stated, promised, and predicted in the Old Testament must happen. He takes it upon himself to guarantee that every detail in the Old Testament will be accomplished.* Far from discarding the Old Testament, Jesus is the active means for the completion of everything in it. The Hebrew Scriptures will happen because of Him. Let's explain this further.

What initiates Jesus' words in Matthew 5:17–18 is the idea that He came to "abolish" or do away with "the Law" and "the Prophets." Jesus' reference to "the Law or the Prophets" comprehensively involves the Hebrew canon as a whole. "Law" is the first five books of Moses—Genesis through Deuteronomy. "Prophets" involves the rest of the Hebrew canon. By mentioning "Law" and "Prophets" together Jesus means the Hebrew Scriptures in their entirety, or what Christians often call the Old Testament. Ten other times in the New Testament "Law" and "Prophets" are coupled to indicate the whole of the Hebrew canon—Matthew 7:12; 11:13; 22:40; Luke 16:16; 24:44; John 1:45; Acts 13:15; 24:14; 28:23; and Romans 3:21. Together, as Grant Osborne rightly observes, "The law or the prophets' means the whole of Scripture."[14] This detail is important for understanding Matthew 5:17–18. The topic at hand is the Hebrew Scriptures as a whole.

Concerning His relationship to the entirety of the Hebrew Scriptures Jesus makes two assertions in 5:17. First, from the negative side, Jesus did not come "to abolish the Law or the Prophets." The word "abolish" is the Greek term *kataluō*, which means "destroy," "demolish," "overthrow," "abolish," or "tear down." Jesus did not come to do away with or get rid of the Old Testament. Any idea that He did is categorically wrong.

Second, from the positive side, Jesus came to "fulfill" the Hebrew Scriptures: "I did not come to abolish but to fulfill." Jesus actively works to fulfill the Old Testament.

We must understand what Jesus meant by "to fulfill" in this context. To do this we examine Matthew's use of "fulfill" in his gospel. And we look at the near context of this section including the key phrase in Matthew 5:18, "until all is accomplished." This explains what it means for Jesus to fulfill the Law and the Prophets.

First, the Greek term for "to fulfill" in Matthew 5:17 is *plērōsai*, coming from the verb, *pleroō*. There are eighty-seven uses of *pleroō* in the New Testament. The term is used in multiple contexts and the meaning of each *pleroō* use must be determined by context. The term can be translated "fulfill," "fullness," "make full," "fill," "complete," "consummate," "realize," "accomplish," "come to pass."

---

14   Grant R. Osborne, *Matthew*, Zondervan Exegetical Commentary on the New Testament (Grand Rapids: Zondervan, 2010), 181.

Pleroō is found sixteen times in Matthew outside of 5:17, with four understandings based on authorial intent in the context:

1. the literal accomplishment of an Old Testament prophecy in its details (1:22; 2:23; 4:14; 8:17; 12:17; 13:35; 21:4; 26:54, 56; 27:9, 35)

2. a correspondence between an event in Israel's history and an event in Jesus' life (2:15, 17)

3. the bringing to fruition of something or making something happen (3:15)

4. a filling to the top or making full (13:48; 23:32)

The dominant meaning of *pleroō* in Matthew is the first option above concerning the literal accomplishment of details of an Old Testament prophecy. And this, most likely, is the meaning in Matthew 5:17. Since Jesus references both "Law" and "Prophets" in 5:17, His intent includes Old Testament prophecies and the Old Testament as a whole. Thus, "to fulfill" in 5:17 concerns the completion or coming to pass of the Old Testament or Hebrew Scriptures.

Second, with 5:18 Jesus explains what He means by "fulfill": "For truly I say to you, until heaven and earth pass away, not the smallest letter or stroke shall pass from the Law until all is accomplished." That verse 18 begins with the term "for" is significant since this word connects verse 17 and verse 18 conceptually. In short, verse 18 explains what Jesus meant by "fulfill" in verse 17. What does Jesus mean by "fulfill" when it comes to the Old Testament? Verse 18 tells us. We do not have to stop with verse 17 and guess what Jesus meant—He tells us what "fulfill" means in the next verse.

When Jesus says, "until heaven and earth pass away," He means the current cosmic order with its "heaven" and "earth." These must remain until everything in the Hebrew Scriptures occurs. The creation cannot give way to the new creation until everything stated and promised in the Old Testament happens. History cannot culminate without everything in the Scriptures occurring. This includes every "letter" and "stroke" found in the Scriptures.

Moving on, Jesus' second use of "Law" in 5:18 is shorthand for "the Law or the Prophets" which He just mentioned in 5:17. This is important to grasp since sometimes people see "Law" in 5:18 and assume Jesus is making a point specifically about the Mosaic Law alone. But "Law" here still refers to the Law and Prophets just mentioned in verse 17. The context of 5:17, with the connecting word "for" in verse 18, indicates that Law and Prophets are still in view. Thus, Jesus refers to the entire Old Testament. If verse 18 is the explanation of verse 17, then the explanation of verse 18 must include the subject of verse 17, which is the entire Old Testament. Plus, we should note that "Law" sometimes refers to the Old Testament as a whole (see Romans 3:19–21). Thus, the context indicates that Jesus is addressing the entire Old Testament with His statement in 5:18. Grasping this is critical for understanding Jesus' main point.

The term "all" in 5:18 refers to *everything* in the Law and the Prophets. So, fulfillment in 5:17 involves "all" or everything in the Hebrew Scriptures. All its predictions. All its covenants. All its prophecies, etc. Again, the scope of Jesus' intent is more than just the Mosaic Law—the entire Scriptures are in view. Since verse 17 is about the Old Testament as a whole, and verse 18 is an explanation of verse 17, verse 18 must involve the Hebrew Scriptures in their entirety.

Next, we come to the strategic word, "accomplished." With
this term we see what Jesus meant by "fulfill" in 5:17. This is
the Greek verb, *genetai*, coming from *ginomai*. In the context
of prophecies or events, *ginomai* carries the idea of "come to
pass" "happen" or "take place" (see Matt. 21:21; 24:6; 26:56).
For example, in the Olivet Discourse Jesus declared that certain
eschatological details must happen: "You will be hearing of
wars and rumors of wars. See that you are not frightened, for
those things must take place (*genesthai*)" (Matt. 24:6, emphases added).

When *ginomai* is used by Jesus concerning prophets
or prophecies, the accomplishment of prophetic details is
His intent. What is predicted must happen as stated. So by
combining "all" with "accomplished" in 5:18—"until all is
accomplished"—Jesus declares that everything stated in the
Hebrew Scriptures must happen. As Wayne Strickland notes,
"That fulfillment of the prophecies of the Old Testament is in
view is signaled by the phrase, 'until everything is accomplished'
in verse 18."[15]

Every letter, every stroke, every word, and every verse of
the Old Testament will happen! All things predicted in the Old
Testament Scriptures must be accomplished in all their details
because Jesus guarantees it. He takes it upon himself to bring
them to completion. As we will discuss soon, since much of
Matthew's gospel involves Jesus fulfilling messianic prophecies,
the accomplishing of messianic prophecies is a major aspect of
what Jesus meant. Commenting on "until all is accomplished"
Vanlaningham states, "the precise idea probably being that

---

15   Wayne G. Strickland, "The Inauguration of the Law of Christ with the Gospel of
      Christ: A Dispensational View," in *The Law, The Gospel, and the Modern Christian:
      Five Views* (Grand Rapids: Zondervan, 1993), 258.

the OT serves as a beacon shining upon Jesus as the one who provides the fulfillment of messianic prophecies."[16]

So how does Matthew 5:17–18 contribute to a proper understanding of how Jesus relates to fulfillment of the Old Testament? *With this passage we learn that Jesus is the means through which the Old Testament in its entirety will be accomplished.*

Jesus does not metaphysically absorb the details of the Old Testament. No vanishing or transformation is found here. He works to complete everything in the Hebrew Scriptures. Much of what we discuss going forward will describe in detail what this completing of Old Testament details means.

Romans 15:8–9: Jesus and the Confirming of Old Testament Promises

Another important text that addresses Jesus and fulfillment of the Old Testament is Romans 15:8–9. Here Paul writes about Jesus' role concerning the accomplishing of Old Testament promises about Israel and the Gentiles:

> For I say that Christ has become a servant to the circumcision on behalf of the truth of God to confirm the promises given to the fathers, and for the Gentiles to glorify God for His mercy; as it is written,

> "Therefore I will give praise to You among
> the Gentiles,
> And I will sing to Your name."

---

16 Michael G. Vanlaningham, "Matthew," in *The Moody Bible Commentary*, eds. Michael Rydelnik and Michael G. Vanlaningham (Chicago: Moody Publishers, 2014), 1461.

Significant here is the statement, "Christ has become a servant to the circumcision on behalf of the truth of God to confirm the promises given to the fathers." This links Jesus and the Old Testament promises. Jesus is a "servant" who has a role to "the circumcision," a reference to Israel. And this role involves confirming promises made to the patriarchs of Israel. And it includes the Servant's mission in bringing blessings to the Gentiles. With this text we see how Jesus relates to God's promises involving Israel and the Gentiles.

Paul's reference to "servant" in verse 8 draws upon the individual Servant concept found in texts like Isaiah 42, 49, 52, and 53. Israel as an entity is God's servant, but there also is an ideal, sinless, individual Servant of God who will save and restore Israel as a corporate entity and bring blessings to the nations (see Isaiah 42, 49). This Servant will bring New Covenant atonement to Israel and nations (see Isaiah 52–53).

With Romans 15:8, Paul focuses on Jesus' Servant role to Israel. Consistent with the Isaiah Servant sections, Paul affirms Jesus as the "servant to the circumcision." Thus, Jesus is a servant of God with a mission to Israel. Jesus does not come to metaphysically absorb the idea of Israel, or make the nation irrelevant. This relates to what was promised in the Old Testament—"on behalf of the truth of God to confirm the promises given to the fathers" (Rom. 15:8). So Paul connects the Servant Jesus with what God promised Israel and the fathers of Israel in the Old Testament.

Jesus' relationship to Israel already was discussed extensively by Paul in Romans 9–11. Even though Israel as a whole was currently in unbelief the Word of God had not failed (see Rom. 9:6a). The covenants, promises, and temple service still belonged to Israel (see Rom. 9:4–5). God has not rejected His people Israel (see Rom. 11:1). Paul also noted that Israel's coming "fullness" and "acceptance" would bring even greater blessings to the world and the nations (see Rom. 11:12, 15). And he declared a coming day when "all Israel will be saved" in 11:26 in connection with the Deliverer—Jesus. Paul then tied this coming reality with Isaiah 59:20–21 which foretold Israel's salvation, the coming of Israel's redeemer, and Israel's inclusion in the New Covenant (see Rom. 11:26–27). Thus, Paul's statement that Jesus came "on behalf of the truth of God" and "to confirm the promises given to the fathers" was well explained in Romans 9–11. Because of the ultimate Israelite—Jesus—the corporate entity of Israel will be saved.

The strategic term Paul used in Romans 15:8 to connect Jesus with Old Testament promises is "confirm." Jesus came to "confirm" the promises of God. The word for "confirm" is *bebaiōsai* which means "to establish" "confirm" "ratify," "secure," "establish," "guarantee." The term carries legal connotations and highlights the formal nature of Jesus' mission to Israel. The Old Testament promised much to Israel in relation to the patriarchs, and Jesus came to "confirm" these promises. Jesus did not come to "transform," "dissolve," or make Old Testament promises "vanish" in Him. He came to "confirm" them—to bring them to completion in all their details, and thus, make good on God's promises to the patriarchs.

Also, since the Servant mentioned in Isaiah also came to bless the Gentiles, Paul links Jesus' confirming ministry with them as well:

> and for the Gentiles to glorify God for His mercy; as it is written,

> "THEREFORE I WILL GIVE PRAISE TO YOU AMONG
>   THE GENTILES,
> AND I WILL SING TO YOUR NAME."

To further his point, with Romans 15:9–12, Paul quoted four Old Testament verses that promised hope for the Gentiles—Psalm 18:49; Deuteronomy 32:43; Psalm 117:1; and Isaiah 11:10. As he does in Romans and his other writings, Paul carefully distinguishes Gentiles from Israel. Gentiles are included as God's people with equal blessings in the Messiah who is the "Root of Jesse," (15:12a), yet Gentiles are Gentiles and Israel is Israel.

Romans 15:8–9, along with Romans 9–11, shows that Paul viewed Jesus, Israel, and Gentiles as three distinct but related entities. Jesus is the ultimate individual Servant, who, as Israel's representative Head, restores corporate Israel. Thus, Jesus' role as the restorer of Israel exists alongside the corporate entity that remains "Israel." Also, Jesus saves the Gentiles as Gentiles. There is no merging of believing Gentiles into Israel.

In sum, the Old Testament predicted a coming individual Servant who would save and restore Israel, and bring light and blessings to the Gentiles. Jesus is the One who does this. Paul's words in Romans 15 are similar to his speech in Acts 26:22–23:

> "So, having obtained help from God, I stand to this day testifying both to small and great, stating nothing but what the Prophets and Moses said was going to take place; that the Christ was to suffer, and that by reason of His resurrection from the dead He would be the first to proclaim light both to the Jewish people and to the Gentiles" (emphases added).

Romans 15:8–9 is significant concerning Jesus and fulfillment of the Old Testament. For Paul, Jesus did not come to absorb, dissolve, or transform the Old Testament promises. Jesus came to confirm and establish them in all their dimensions for both Israel and the Gentiles.

Matthew 3:15

A strategic statement concerning Jesus and fulfillment is found in Matthew 3:15b. In response to John the Baptist's hesitancy to baptize Jesus, Jesus said, "Allow it at this time; for in this way it is fitting for us to fulfill all righteousness." Jesus declares that John and He are linked with the fulfilling of all righteousness. What is the meaning and significance of this?

Jesus does not say what fulfilling all righteousness specifically means. And there are several different views of this statement. So caution must be used when speculating on this verse. But how does this verse relate to Jesus and fulfillment?

Many have noted that Jesus is being introduced to Israel. That is true. And He is humbly identifying with His people. That too is likely. The baptism also launches Jesus' formal adult ministry. But more is happening. We believe the fulfillment of all righteousness relates primarily to the kingdom of heaven and the roles Jesus and John have concerning the kingdom. John prepares the way for the King in fulfillment of Isaiah 40:3 and Malachi 3:1, and Jesus is the King who brings the kingdom predicted in the Old Testament prophets. The road to that will involve Jesus' teachings, death, resurrection, judgments, and actual kingdom establishment at His return. But let's discuss this further.

The theme of Matthew's gospel is the kingdom of heaven and Jesus as King. Matthew 1:1a links Jesus as "the son of David." Plus, the overall message of both John the Baptist and Jesus was the kingdom and the repentance needed to enter the kingdom:

> Now in those days John the Baptist came, preaching in the wilderness of Judea, saying, "Repent, for the kingdom of heaven is at hand" (Matt. 3:1–2).

> From that time Jesus began to preach and say, "Repent, for
> the kingdom of heaven is at hand" (Matt. 4:17).

The kingdom was not just one of many things John and Jesus
were discussing, it was their main message.

The "kingdom" in Matthew and the New Testament
includes individual salvation, but it also is more than that. The
kingdom proclaimed by the Old Testament prophets, Jesus, and
the apostles is the earthly kingdom of the Messiah over Israel,
the nations, and all creation. The kingdom that transforms all
areas of reality—social, cultural, and political. The kingdom
that brings physical healing and resurrection. There are spiritual
elements too. This is a righteous and just kingdom of which one
must be born again to enter (see John 3:3). But it also is a power-
ful earthly kingdom that replaces the geo-political empires that
preceded it (see Daniel 2 and 7).

Thus, the fulfilling of all righteousness probably relates to
the kingdom of heaven that Jesus will establish on the earth, and
all this entails. This is probably linked with the "restoration of
all things" that Peter said Jesus would bring with Jesus' return
to earth at His second advent (see Acts 3:20–21). John, too, has
a secondary role in the kingdom's establishment since he is the
forerunner of the King and the one calling on people to repent in
light of the nearness of the kingdom.

Implications also exist for Jesus' followers. The terms "righteous" and "righteousness" occur twenty-three times in Matthew.
Many of these discuss righteous people (i.e. Jesus followers)
entering the kingdom of heaven:

> "Blessed are those who have been persecuted for the sake
> of righteousness, for theirs is the kingdom of heaven"
> (Matt. 5:10).

"For I say to you that unless your righteousness far surpasses that of the scribes and Pharisees, you will not enter the kingdom of heaven" (Matt. 5:20).

Then the righteous will shine forth like the sun in the kingdom of their Father" (Matt. 13:43a).

"These will go away into eternal punishment, but the righteous into eternal life" (Matt. 25:46).

With Matthew 3:15, the fulfilling of all righteousness refers to the roles Jesus and John have in bringing about the righteous kingdom of heaven to earth and the salvation needed for people to enter it. John prepared the way for Jesus and Jesus is the One who will bring the kingdom and baptize His followers with the Holy Spirit. Jesus' baptism by John inaugurated the official ministry of Jesus and the road to the kingdom of heaven.

Summary

Jesus is central to all God's purposes for all creation. And Jesus works in such a way that all of God's creational, kingdom, covenant, salvation, and historical purposes will happen in all their dimensions. This involves everything concerning the universe, earth, land, Israel, nations, spiritual blessings, physical blessings, etc.!

Also, since there are two comings of Jesus, fulfillment of God's purposes will occur in stages. Some fulfillments of Old Testament promises occurred with Jesus' first coming, yet other fulfillments await completion at Jesus' return. But in the end, everything God promised and predicted will take place because of Jesus. As Paul stated in 2 Corinthians 1:20: "For as many as are the promises of God, in Him they are yes."

CHAPTER FOUR

JESUS AND THE ACCOMPLISHING OF MESSIANIC PROPHECIES

Jesus is the means for the fulfillment of the Old Testament. Now we discuss specific ways Jesus fulfills the Old Testament. One major way Jesus fulfills the Old Testament is by directly accomplishing the details of messianic prophecies about himself. To clarify, a messianic prophecy involves a prediction in the Old Testament concerning a coming special Person who will be a King, Warrior, Savior, Prophet, Priest, etc. Jesus is the One who fulfills such specific messianic prophecies. Below are several examples of this type of fulfillment.

Luke 24:25–27; 44–47 and the Sufferings of the Messiah

According to Luke 24:25–27, Jesus told the men heading to Emmaus, after His resurrection, that He fulfilled Old Testament prophecies that predicted His suffering and glory:

> And He said to them, "O foolish men and slow of heart to believe in all that the prophets have spoken! Was it not necessary for the Christ to suffer these things and to enter into His glory?" Then beginning with Moses and with all the prophets, He explained to them the things concerning Himself in all the Scriptures.

Then with Luke 24:44–47 Jesus told the apostles that He fulfilled what the Scriptures predicted about His suffering, resurrection, and the Gospel being proclaimed to the nations:

> Now He said to them, "These are My words which I spoke to you while I was still with you, that all things which are written about Me in the Law of Moses and the Prophets and the Psalms must be fulfilled." Then He opened their minds to understand the Scriptures, and He said to them, "Thus it is written, that the Christ would suffer and rise again from the dead the third day, and that repentance for forgiveness of sins would be proclaimed in His name to all the nations, beginning from Jerusalem."

These passages in Luke 24 reveal two important things. First, Jesus viewed His actions of suffering and resurrection as the direct, literal fulfillment and completion of what the Old Testament Scriptures explicitly predicted. And second, the content of fulfillment He focused upon involved: (1) His sufferings; (2) His resurrection; (3) His entering glory; and (4) the Gospel now being universally proclaimed.

We are not told which specific Old Testament passages Jesus cited as "He explained to them the things concerning Himself in all the Scriptures" (Luke 24:27). He certainly had a wide array of passages to choose from since there are so many messianic prophecies in the Old Testament. Perhaps He cited texts like Genesis 3:15 that spoke of a coming seed of the woman who would defeat evil. Maybe He quoted Isaiah 52–53 which predicted that the coming Servant would atone for the sins of Israel and sprinkle many nations with His New Covenant atonement (Isa. 52:15). These texts, and many others, predicted the things that Jesus said He fulfilled. Regardless, Jesus declared that He literally completed Old Testament messianic prophecies about His sufferings and glory.

Because some have misunderstood this text, Jesus is not saying every Old Testament passage directly refers to himself. But He does say that all things that the Hebrew Scriptures stated about Him must be fulfilled by Him.

Matthew 2:5–6 / Micah 5:2 and the Messiah's Birth in Bethlehem

According to Matthew 2:5–6, Jesus literally fulfilled the prophecy of Micah 5:2 that the Messiah would be born in Bethlehem. When Herod asked the Magi about Jesus' whereabouts, we are told:

> They said to him, "In Bethlehem of Judea; for this is what has been written by the prophet:
>
> 'And you, Bethlehem, land of Judah,
> Are by no means least among the leaders of Judah;
> For out of you shall come forth a Ruler
> Who will shepherd My people Israel.'"

Jesus fulfilled the prophecy concerning the Messiah's birth in Bethlehem.

Matthew 4:13–16 / Isaiah 9:1–2 and the Messiah Preaching Good News to Northern Israel

Matthew viewed Jesus' geographical movement in Matthew 4 to be the fulfillment of parts of Isaiah 9. Isaiah 9 not only discussed the coming of the Messiah (see 9:6–7), but also good news for Zebulun, Naphtali, and nearby Gentiles. Isaiah 9:1a says gloom would be removed from Israel, and "the land of Zebulun and the land of Naphtali," which experienced "contempt," would be made "glorious." Matthew then quoted Isaiah 9:1–2 concerning Jesus' northern travels:

> This was to fulfill what was spoken through Isaiah the
>   prophet:
> "The land of Zebulun and the land of Naphtali,
>   By the way of the sea,
>   beyond the Jordan, Galilee of the Gentiles—
> "The people who were sitting in darkness saw a
>   great Light,
>   And those who were sitting in the land and
>   shadow of death,
> Upon them a Light dawned" (Matt. 4:14–16).

Jesus' coming to Zebulun and Naphtali in connection with a message of kingdom hope to Israel with implications for Gentiles is a direct literal fulfillment of Isaiah 9:1–2.

Matthew 21:4–5; John 12:13–15 / Zechariah 9:9 and the Messiah Coming to Jerusalem on a Donkey

Zechariah 9:9 predicted the Messiah would come to Jerusalem on a donkey in a humble manner. Jesus fulfilled this prophecy with His entrance into Jerusalem on Palm Sunday:

> This took place to fulfill what was spoken through
>   the prophet:
> "Say to the daughter of Zion,
> 'Behold your King is coming to you,
> Gentle, and mounted on a donkey,
> Even on a colt, the foal of a beast of burden'"
> (Matt. 21:4–5; cf. John 12:13–15).

Luke 4:17–19 / Isaiah 61:1–2 and Good News

Isaiah 61 foretold an anointed Person with God's Spirit upon Him who will bring salvation and restoration to Israel, including rebuilt cities and "an everlasting covenant" (i.e. New Covenant). According to verses 1–2a this person will preach the Gospel to the poor, release captives, give sight to the blind, free the oppressed, and proclaim the favorable year of the Lord. Centuries later at a synagogue in Nazareth, Jesus stood up and read Isaiah 61:1–2a and declared that this passage was fulfilled with Him: "Today this Scripture has been fulfilled in your hearing" (Luke 4:21). Isaiah 61 is a messianic passage about what the Messiah would do for Israel, and Jesus viewed Isaiah 61:1–2a as being fulfilled by Him. Jesus did not quote verse 2b which speaks of the day of God's vengeance. That will be fulfilled with Jesus' second coming. Nevertheless, Jesus' first coming brought fulfillment of Isaiah 61:1–2a.

Mark 15:27–28 / Isaiah 53:12b and Being Numbered with Transgressors

Isaiah 53:12b declared that the Servant would be numbered with transgressors in His suffering. Jesus fulfilled this by being crucified between two criminals:

> They crucified two robbers with Him, one on His right and one on His left. And the Scripture was fulfilled which says, "And He was numbered with transgressors" (Mark 15:27–28)

Acts 2:27 / Psalm 16:10 and the Messiah's Predicted Resurrection

With Psalm 16:10 David declared that the coming "Holy One" of God (i.e. the Messiah) would not undergo decay in the grave:

> For You will not abandon my soul to Sheol;
> You will not allow Your Holy One to undergo decay.

With Acts 2:27, Peter quoted Psalm 16:10 when making his argument in Jerusalem that Jesus must be resurrected from the dead. He then offered commentary on what David meant in Psalm 16:10:

> So because he [David] was a prophet and knew that God had sworn to him with an oath to seat one of his descendants on

his throne, he looked ahead and spoke of the resurrection of the Christ, that He was neither abandoned to Hades, nor did His flesh suffer decay. It is this Jesus whom God raised up (Acts 2:30–32a)

Peter explained that David predicted the resurrection of God's Holy One. So David explicitly predicted the resurrection of Jesus.

Many other examples of this type of fulfillment—literal fulfillment of messianic prophecies—exist. But now we move to a second way that Jesus fulfills the Old Testament—the completion of messianic hope expectations.

CHAPTER FIVE

JESUS AND THE COMPLETION OF MESSIANIC HOPE EXPECTATIONS

E arly in John's gospel Philip declared to Nathanael: "We have found Him of whom Moses in the Law and also the Prophets wrote—Jesus of Nazareth, the son of Joseph" (John 1:45). Philip rightly noted that Jesus is the specific Person that Moses and the Prophets wrote about. Jesus is the completion of their messianic hope expectations. So not only does Jesus fulfill specific prophecies about the Messiah, as we noted in the previous chapter, but He also fulfills Old Testament expectations concerning a special Person who would fulfill God's purposes. Below we list several messianic hope expectations that find fulfillment with Jesus.

Defeater of Satan and Evil

With Genesis 3 a nefarious serpent tempted the first image-bearers to disobey God. He succeeded in his mission, but his victory will not stand forever. The first messianic prophecy is found in Genesis 3:15 where God promised a coming "seed" from the woman who would defeat evil and crush the serpent:

> "And I will put enmity
> Between you and the woman,

And between your seed and her seed;
He shall bruise you on the head,
And you shall bruise him on the heel."

This "seed" of the woman culminates in Jesus who through His two comings crushes Satan and puts an end of evil. Jesus inflicted a fatal wound to Satan at the cross as He broke the power of sin and death. And the final defeat of Satan will occur with Satan's confinement in the abyss and eventual casting into the lake of fire (cf. Rom. 16:20; Rev. 20:1-10). Paul stated in Romans 16:20 that, "The God of peace will soon crush Satan under your feet." Thus, one of the primary roles of Jesus is that of Defeater of Satan and Evil.

Curse-Remover / Restorer of Creation

When Adam sinned the ground was cursed. The ground Adam was supposed to rule over would now work against him.

"Cursed is the ground because of you;
In toil you will eat of it
All the days of your life.
Both thorns and thistles it shall grow for you;
And you will eat the plants of the field" (Gen. 3:17b–18).

But God offered hope to this dismal development. A second messianic hope text is Genesis 5:28–29 which expresses hope that someone will remove the curse upon the ground:

Lamech lived one hundred and eighty-two years, and became the father of a son. Now he called his name Noah, saying, "This one will give us rest from our work and from the toil of our hands arising from the ground which the Lord has cursed."

Lamech hoped for "rest from our work and from the toil of our hand" stemming from the curse. His desire that Noah would be this curse-remover is significant. We know Noah was used by God with the flood of Noah's day, but Noah was not the One who would remove the curse upon the ground. But Lamech presents a messianic hope expectation for removal of the curse upon the ground.

Jesus is the One who will ultimately fulfill this expectation. Jesus is the One who will restore creation and remove the curse, as Romans 8:19–21 indicates:

> For the anxious longing of the creation waits eagerly for the revealing of the sons of God. For the creation was subjected to futility, not willingly, but because of Him who subjected it, in hope that the creation itself also will be set free from its slavery to corruption into the freedom of the glory of the children of God.

Isaiah 11:6–9 is a messianic text about the Messiah restoring the animal realm to peace within itself and with humanity:

> And the wolf will dwell with the lamb,
> And the leopard will lie down with the young goat,
> And the calf and the young lion and the fatling together;
> And a little boy will lead them.
> Also the cow and the bear will graze,
> Their young will lie down together,
> And the lion will eat straw like the ox.
> The nursing child will play by the hole of the cobra,

And the weaned child will put his hand on the viper's den.
They will not hurt or destroy in all My holy mountain,
For the earth will be full of the knowledge of the Lord
As the waters cover the sea.

The original kingdom mandate for man was to rule the earth and its creatures (see Gen. 1:26, 28). Adam even named the animals showing his dominion over them. Since the fall the animal realm has worked against mankind. The creatures too have suffered from man's sin, fall, and the curse. But Jesus, the Last Adam, will rule the earth and restore the animal realm just as this Isaiah text stated.

Ruler of Nations

Several messianic hope texts in the Old Testament predict a coming Ruler of nations. According to Genesis 49:10 the coming "Shiloh" will rule the earth and be obeyed by the peoples on earth:

"The scepter shall not depart from Judah,
Nor the ruler's staff from between his feet,
Until Shiloh comes,
And to him shall be the obedience of the peoples."

With Psalm 2:6–9 the LORD says He will give His Son, the Messiah, the nations as His inheritance:

"But as for Me, I have installed My King
Upon Zion, My holy mountain."
"I will surely tell of the decree of the Lord:
He said to Me, 'You are My Son,
Today I have begotten You.

'Ask of Me, and I will surely give the nations as Your
    inheritance,
And the very ends of the earth as Your possession.
'You shall break them with a rod of iron,
You shall shatter them like earthenware.'"

Psalm 110:1–2 presents the Messiah as having a session at the right hand of God in heaven until the time comes for the Messiah to reign from Jerusalem:

The LORD says to my Lord:
"Sit at My right hand
Until I make Your enemies a footstool for Your feet."
The LORD will stretch forth Your strong scepter from
    Zion, saying,
"Rule in the midst of Your enemies."

This involves the judging of nations:

He will shatter kings in the day of His wrath.
He will judge among the nations (Psalm 110:5b–6a).

Jesus is this Ruler who will rule over the nations. Revelation 1:5 calls Jesus, "the ruler of the kings of the earth." And He will act as Ruler of nations at His second coming. In Matthew 25:31–32 Jesus states:

"But when the Son of Man comes in His glory, and all the angels with Him, then He will sit on His glorious throne. All the nations will be gathered before Him; and He will separate them from one another, as the shepherd separates the sheep from the goats."

Revelation 19:15a also declares that Jesus will rule the nations as a result of His second coming:

> From His mouth comes a sharp sword, so that with it He may strike down the nations, and He will rule them with a rod of iron.

The Old Testament presents messianic expectations for a coming ruler over nations—not just to save people from nations, but to rule geo-political nations. Jesus will fulfill this messianic hope following His second coming to earth.

Last Adam

The Bible contrasts the roles of the two representatives of humanity—Adam and Jesus. The first Adam represented mankind but Adam failed in his relationship with God. Adam also failed the kingdom mandate from God to rule and subdue the earth successfully for God's glory (see Gen. 1:26, 28). All humanity since Adam has failed too. But Jesus is the Last Adam, the ideal King and ultimate representative of mankind. And He succeeds where Adam failed.

There are four main ways that Jesus succeeds where the first Adam did not. First, Adam failed the temptation test of Genesis 3. But Jesus triumphed over Satan's temptation in the wilderness according to Matthew 4:1–11.

Second, Jesus brings justification and life to those in union with Him in contrast to Adam who brought condemnation and death to all. This is Paul's main point of Romans 5:12–21 when He compares how both Adam and Jesus impact humanity.

Third, because of sin Adam's body (and ours) is linked with corruption and death. Jesus, though, brings resurrection of the body (1 Corinthians 15:42–49).

Fourth, Jesus will successfully complete the kingdom mandate first given to Adam (see Gen. 1:26, 28; Psalm 8; Heb. 2:5–9). Adam was tasked to rule and subdue the earth as God's mediator. He failed. But Jesus will succeed by ruling and subduing the earth when He returns. According to 1 Corinthians 15:24–25, the transition to the eternal kingdom results from Jesus' successful reign:

> then comes the end, when He hands over the kingdom to our God and Father, when He has abolished all rule and all authority and power. For He must reign until He has put all His enemies under His feet.

So Jesus is the One who fulfills the kingdom task first given to Adam to rule and subdue the earth and its creatures. And when He does this successfully, a transition occurs to the eternal kingdom (cf. Revelation 21 and 22). Jesus completes everything God intended for humanity. And for those who in union with Jesus, they, too, succeed and benefit in everything the Last Adam accomplishes.

Seed of Abraham

The Abrahamic Covenant is the foundational covenant of promise. From it stems the other covenants of promise—Davidic and New. The Abrahamic Covenant has many dimensions. These include promises related to Abraham, Isaac, and Jacob; the nation Israel; the families and nations of the earth; physical blessings, spiritual blessings, etc.

The seed of Abraham concept is broad with several dimensions. First, it includes the special physical seed line through Abraham, Isaac, and Jacob—culminating in the nation of Israel.

Second, there is a non-special physical seed line of natural descendants such as Ishmael from Hagar and the sons Abraham had with Keturah. Third, there is a spiritual seed of Abraham, which refers to all believers in God through faith alone, regardless of ethnicity. And fourth, there is Jesus, who is the ultimate individual Seed of Abraham and the center of the seed of Abraham concept. Galatians 3:16 states: "Now the promises were spoken to Abraham and to his seed. He does not say, 'And to seeds,' as one would in referring to many, but rather as in referring to one, 'And to your seed,' that is, Christ."

Because of Jesus all dimensions of the Abrahamic Covenant will be completed. This includes national promises to Israel. Mary declared that her Son Jesus would bring help to Israel based on what God promised Abraham:

> "He has given help to Israel His servant,
> In remembrance of His mercy,
> As He spoke to our fathers,
> To Abraham and his descendants [lit. "seed"] forever"
> (Luke 1:54–55).

According to the prophecy of Luke 1, Jesus is the One who will deliver Israel from her enemies, in fulfillment of the oath God made to Abraham:

> "To show mercy toward our fathers,
> And to remember His holy covenant,
> The oath which He swore to Abraham our father,
> To grant us that we, being rescued from the hand of
>   our enemies,
> Might serve Him without fear" (Luke 1:67–74).

Gentile blessing is also part of the Abrahamic Covenant. With Genesis 12:2–3 God told Abraham that through him and the nation Israel, "all the families of the earth will be blessed." Jesus is the One who brings messianic salvation to the Gentiles. Galatians 3:6–9 states:

> Even so Abraham believed God, and it was reckoned to him as righteousness. Therefore, be sure that it is those who are of faith who are sons of Abraham. The Scripture, foreseeing that God would justify the Gentiles by faith, preached the gospel beforehand to Abraham, saying, "All the nations will be blessed in you." So then those who are of faith are blessed with Abraham, the believer.

The fulfillment of the Abrahamic Covenant only occurs in all its dimensions through the ultimate singular seed of Abraham— Jesus—who accomplishes all dimensions of the Abrahamic Covenant. This includes the promise that Israel would be permanently delivered from her enemies and for Gentiles to be blessed through Abraham and Israel (see Gen. 22:17–18; Gal. 3:16, 29).

Davidic King / Messiah

Jesus is the ultimate Davidic King and Messiah who will (1) rule over Israel forever (Luke 1:31–33); (2) judge the nations from David's throne (Matt. 25:31–32); (3) restore creation (Matt. 19:28–29); and (4) and bring messianic salvation to believing Gentiles (see Acts 15:13–18). Jesus, the ultimate Davidic King is also the One who transitions us from the Mosaic era to the New Covenant era (Luke 22:20).

The first verse of the New Testament links Jesus with David: "The record of the genealogy of Jesus the Messiah, the son of David, the son of Abraham" (Matt. 1:1). Jesus is at the center of the Davidic Covenant, and He is the One who will have the ultimate kingdom reign. In Zechariah 14:9, we are told, "And the Lord will be king over all the earth; in that day, the Lord will be the only one, and his name the only one." Revelation 19:15 states, "From his mouth comes a sharp sword, so that with it he may strike down the nations, and he will rule them with a rod of iron." So there are many passages in Scripture, both Old Testament and New Testament, that predict that Jesus is going to fulfill the Genesis 1 mandate. He is going to rule the earth, its creatures, and He is also going to rule the nations of the earth.

In Chapter 7 we will discuss in more detail how the New Testament connects Jesus as the ultimate David.

Prophet

In Deuteronomy 18:15 Moses predicted a coming Prophet to whom the people of Israel would listen: "The LORD your God will raise up for you a prophet like me from among you, from your countrymen, you shall listen to him." Jesus is the fulfillment of this prophet like Moses. John 6:15 states: "Therefore when the people saw the sign which He [Jesus] had performed, they said, 'This is truly the Prophet who is to come into the world.'" Then John 7:40 states: "Some of the people therefore, when they heard these words, were saying, 'This certainly is the Prophet.'"

With Acts 3:20 Peter says Jesus is the Messiah appointed for Israel. Then Peter mentions Deuteronomy 18:15 and Moses' prediction about a coming prophet in reference to Jesus:

> [Jesus] whom heaven must receive until the period of resto-
> ration of all things about which God spoke by the mouth
> of His holy prophets from ancient time. Moses said, "THE

Lord God will raise up for you a prophet like me from your brethren; to Him you shall give heed to everything He says to you. And it will be that every soul that does not heed that prophet shall be utterly destroyed from among the people" (Acts 3:21–23).

Priest

Priests mediate God's presence to others. While various priests have existed in biblical history, Jesus is the ultimate Priest. Psalm 110 presents the Messiah as seated at Yahweh's right hand for a time until Yahweh sends the Messiah to defeat and rule the nations from Jerusalem (see Ps. 110:1–2). Yet, with Psalm 110:4 we also see that the Davidic King at God's right hand is also a Priest:

> The Lord has sworn and will not change His mind,
> "You are a priest forever
> According to the order of Melchizedek."

According to the Mosaic Covenant, the Davidic kings were not priests. But the Messiah is both King and Priest. And as verse 4 states, He is "a priest according to the order of Melchizedek." No person before Jesus ever met the conditions of Psalm 110 with its King-Priest who has a session at God's right hand before He reigns over the earth.

Yet the Book of Hebrews tells us that Jesus is the fulfillment of the Psalm 110:4 Priest who is in the order of Melchizedek.

> [Jesus] being designated by God as a high priest according to the order of Melchizedek (Heb. 5:10).

where Jesus has entered as a forerunner for us, having become a high priest forever according to the order of Melchizedek (Heb. 6:20).

As a result of His death, resurrection, and ascension, Jesus is the fulfillment of the Psalm 110 Priest in the order of Melchizedek.

Suffering Servant

Another major messianic hope role Jesus fulfills is that of the Suffering Servant of Isaiah 52 and 53. When John the Baptist saw Jesus coming towards him he declared, "Behold, the Lamb of God who takes away the sin of the world!" (John 1:29b). This truth of Jesus being a Lamb who takes away sin for Israel and the nations was foretold in Isaiah's depiction of the Suffering Servant. Isaiah 53 predicted a coming Suffering Servant who would be "Like a lamb that is led to slaughter" (53:7b). This Servant would be without sin or blemish. In a substitutionary manner He would atone for the sins of Israel and also "sprinkle many nations" [i.e. Gentiles] (Isa. 52:15) with His New Covenant sacrifice.

The New Testament presents Jesus as the literal fulfillment of this Servant in Isaiah 53. At the Last Supper, Jesus declared that He fulfilled Isaiah 53:12b: "For I tell you that this which is written must be fulfilled in Me, 'And He was numbered with transgressors'; for that which refers to Me has its fulfillment" (Luke 22:37).

Jesus also fulfilled the Isaiah 53:4 prediction of the Servant taking infirmities and diseases upon himself: "This was to fulfill what was spoken through Isaiah the prophet: 'He Himself took our infirmities and carried away our diseases'" (Matt. 8:17).

With his speech to the "men of Israel" (Acts 3:12) Peter declared Jesus' role as the fulfiller of a suffering ministry: "But the things which God announced beforehand by the mouth of all the prophets, that His Christ would suffer, He has thus fulfilled" (Acts 3:18).

In Acts 8, Philip found an Ethiopian sitting in a chariot reading Isaiah 53:7–8, a text predicting the Suffering Servant's role in dying for sins:

> Now the passage of Scripture which he was reading was this: "He was led as a sheep to slaughter; And as a lamb before its shearer is silent, So He does not open His mouth. In humiliation His judgment was taken away; Who will relate His generation? For His life is removed from the earth" (Acts 8:32–33).

The Ethiopian asked Philip who this referred to, and Philip answered that this spoke of Jesus:

> The eunuch answered Philip and said, "Please tell me, of whom does the prophet say this? Of himself or of someone else?" Then Philip opened his mouth, and beginning from this Scripture he preached Jesus to him. (Acts 8:34–35)[17]

Jesus is the One who fulfills the hope of a coming Suffering Servant who would atone for the sins of Israel and the nations.

---

17   Other connections of Jesus with the Servant of Isaiah 53 are found with John 12:38 (Isa. 53:1); Romans 10:16 (Isa. 53:1); and 1 Peter 2:22-25 (Isa. 53:9).

Savior and Restorer of Israel

The nation Israel has a major role in Scripture. According to Genesis 12:2–3 Israel has a role in blessing "all the families of the earth" and "all the nations of the earth" (cf. 18:18). Yet as predicted in texts like Deuteronomy 30 and Leviticus 26, Israel would disobey God and need salvation itself. Thus, another important Messianic Hope role in the Old Testament concerns a special Person who will be the Savior and Restorer of Israel.

While the nation Israel is presented as a servant of God in the Old Testament, several chapters in Isaiah predicted a coming individual Servant who would save and restore the sinful nation. This individual Servant of Israel is described in Isaiah 49:3:

> He said to Me, "You are My Servant, Israel,
> In Whom I will show My glory."

Then with 49:5a, this perfect individual Servant speaks of His God-given task to save and gather wayward Israel back to God:

> And now says the Lord, who formed Me from the womb to
> be His Servant, To bring Jacob back to Him, so that Israel
> might be gathered to Him.

49:6a then mentions the Servant's role in raising up the tribes of Israel and restoring Israel:

> He says, "It is too small a thing that You should be
>   My Servant
> To raise up the tribes of Jacob and to restore the preserved
>   ones of Israel."

Note the relationship between the individual Servant of Israel and the corporate entity of Israel. The individual Servant has a God-given role to the sinful corporate entity. This Servant, who is the ultimate Israelite, will save, gather, and restore the nation Israel. The One restores the many.

The Servant of Israel will also bring the New Covenant to Israel and will restore the land to Israel, according to Isaiah 49:8b:

> "And I will keep You and give You for a covenant of
>   the people,
> To restore the land, to make them inherit the desolate
>   heritages."

The New Testament presents Jesus as this Servant who will save and restore Israel. With Romans 15:8 Paul calls Jesus the "servant to the circumcision" who fulfills God's promises to Israel's patriarchs: "For I say that Christ has become a servant to the circumcision on behalf of the truth of God to confirm the promises given to the fathers."

In predicting the coming of Jesus an angel declared: "She [Mary] will bear a Son; and you shall call His name Jesus, for He will save His people [Israel] from their sins." In Luke 1:54, Mary explains that God will help His servant, Israel:

> "He has given help to Israel His servant,
> In remembrance of His mercy...."

With his speech to the "men of Israel" in Jerusalem (Acts 3:12), Peter said God raised up Jesus, His Servant, to bless Israel: "For you first [Israel], God raised up His Servant and sent Him to bless you by turning every one of you from your wicked ways"

(Acts 3:26). Peter says Jesus is God's Servant who brings salvation to Israel.

Isaiah 49 explicitly stated that the individual Servant of Israel will save, regather, and restore national Israel. But the Servant's role does not stop with Israel. Isaiah 49:6b states the Servant will save the "nations" of the earth:

> "I will also make You a light of the nations
> So that My salvation may reach to the end of the earth."

In Luke 2:32 Simeon draws upon the truths of Isaiah 49 when he declared that Mary's Son, Jesus, would be:

> "A Light of revelation to the Gentiles,
> And the glory of Your people Israel."

Thus, one major role Jesus must fulfill is Savior and Restorer of Israel. The basis for Israel's salvation exists with Jesus' death and Suffering Servant role. Yet Romans 11:26 also predicts a coming salvation of "all Israel" that will occur in the future.

CHAPTER SIX

JESUS AND THE REALIZATION OF ISRAEL'S EXODUS FROM EXILE

"The hopes and fears of all the years
are met in thee tonight."

You might recognize this great line from the famous Christmas carol, "O Little Town of Bethlehem," by Phillips Brooks. It captures the truth that the hopes and fears of mankind found their culmination with Jesus' birth in Bethlehem. Since the fall of Genesis 3, man's state has been that of turmoil, suffering, and death. God offered hope in Genesis 3:15 that a special "seed" or representative of mankind would defeat evil and save humanity. Yet as the centuries passed, this hope went unrealized. But on that historic night in Bethlehem, when Jesus was born, the hopes and fears of God's people throughout history, indeed, were met in Him.

This fulfillment in Jesus was not mystical. It did not occur with a snap of the fingers. History did not end that night. Nor did all of God's plans happen that day. Jesus' sufferings and kingdom glory still had to happen. But truly, on that first Christmas night, something was completed in Jesus. In Jesus' face existed the hope of Israel, humanity, and all creation.

This idea that Jesus is the culmination of Israel's hopes and fears is present with two strategic quotations of the Old

Testament in Matthew: Matthew 2:14–15/Hosea 11:1 and Matthew 2:17–19/Jeremiah 31:15. Here Matthew uses the fulfillment word—*pleroō*—in a nuanced manner to show Jesus is linked with Israel's history, both in tragedy and in hope. History will repeat itself with events in Jesus' life to highlight that He is the ultimate Israelite and Son, the One who can save and restore Israel, bring blessings to all nations, and heal all creation.

Jesus the Corporate Head of Israel

The Israelites of biblical times were not only interested in the literal fulfillment of biblical prophecies, they also looked for patterns and connections between persons and events. Key events and figures in Israel's history could point to even greater events and persons. The people also understood the concept of corporate solidarity or corporate representation in which a special "one" can represent the "many." And the experiences of the "one" also could relate to the experiences of the group. Such a connection is not always as familiar to modern Western audiences, but it was to ancient Jewish readers. As Craig Blomberg notes, "For believing Jews, merely to discern striking parallels between God's actions in history, especially in decisive moments of revelation and redemption, could convince them of divinely intended 'coincidence.'"[18]

As we will see, fulfillment in Jesus can relate to Jesus completing and being the hero of Israel's story. As Israel's representative Head, Jesus, through His two comings, brings Israel's sufferings and tragedies to an end. He brings restoration and the

---

18 Craig L. Blomberg, "Matthew," in *Commentary on the New Testament Use of the Old Testament*, eds. G. K. Beale and D. A. Carson (Grand Rapids: Baker, 2007), 8. I am not claiming Blomberg is an advocate of single-meaning use of the OT.

realization of Israel's hope. As this happens, He also brings healing and restoration to the world.

So another way Jesus fulfills the Old Testament involves His connection or relationship with previous events in history. Events in Jesus' life sometimes correspond to events in Israel's history to show that God's plans to save and restore Israel center on the person and work of Jesus. This is especially true when the Old Testament passages being quoted contain a messianic hope expectation, which we find with the two examples below. With these we see historical correspondences between Israel and Jesus in the context of messianic hope to let us know that Israel's exile and hope for another exodus will occur because of Jesus.

Matthew 2:14–15 / Hosea 11:1

Our first example involves the connection between Israel's exodus from Egypt under Moses as God's son, and a coming second exodus for Israel led by the ultimate Son and Israelite—Jesus. We find this with Matthew's quotation of Hosea 11:1 in Matthew 2:14–15:

> So Joseph got up and took the Child and His mother while it was still night, and left for Egypt. He remained there until the death of Herod. This was to fulfill what had been spoken by the Lord through the prophet: "Out of Egypt I called My Son."

God calling Jesus out of Egypt is said to "fulfill" God's calling Israel from Egypt. Matthew connects Jesus' "exodus-from-Egypt" experience as God's Son with Israel's "exodus-from-Egypt" experience as God's son hundreds of years earlier. Note the points of comparison:

+   Israel as God's son corresponds to Jesus as God's Son.

+   Israel being called out of Egypt corresponds to Jesus being called out of Egypt.

The significance of this quotation of Hosea 11:1 in Matthew 2:15 has been much debated. Some think Matthew is quoting Hosea 11:1 out of context or redefining what "fulfill" means since a historical statement about Israel's exodus from Egypt supposedly cannot be a prophecy about Jesus leaving Egypt. How could Jesus coming out of Egypt be a literal fulfillment of Israel's historical exodus from Egypt seven hundred years earlier? Hosea 11:1 allegedly cannot be fulfilled in Jesus because it refers to a past historical event and Hosea was not predicting anything about Jesus. To say Hosea intentionally had Jesus in mind with this verse is absurd, or so some think. So when Matthew quotes Hosea 11:1 he is quoting this text noncontextually.

As you can probably detect, we disagree with this understanding. We believe Hosea was looking forward to the Messiah, and Hosea's reference to the historical exodus has contextual correspondence to what God is doing through Jesus since the book of Hosea explicitly predicted a coming Davidic King who would restore Israel with an exodus event. Matthew rightly notes that Jesus fulfills the expectation of Hosea. Thus, when Matthew 2:15 quotes Hosea 11:1, and links its fulfillment with Jesus, this is a contextual use of the Old Testament.

Let us explain further. When looking at the issue of Old Testament fulfillment, one must know the Old Testament context of a verse(s) quoted. One must pay attention to authorial logic and the overall argument an author is making. Every statement in the Hebrew Scriptures has a context and is part of a broader argument an author is conveying. When some think Matthew 2:15 is quoting Hosea 11:1 out of context, they often are not understanding the context of the book of Hosea or Hosea's point in 11:1 specifically. When the context of Hosea as a book is rightly grasped, one will see what Hosea was doing in Hosea 11:1 and that Matthew quoted Hosea 11:1 contextually in Matthew 2:15. There is a direct fulfillment between what Hosea intended and what Matthew says was being accomplished with Jesus.

So let us look at the authorial logic of Hosea. One key argument of Hosea is that a coming Davidic King (i.e. Messiah) will rescue the nation Israel from exile with a second exodus. This involves salvation and restoration to the land of promise with spiritual and physical blessings. For example, Hosea 3:4–5 explicitly predicted an extended exile for Israel, but afterwards the coming Davidic King will reverse the exile and save and restore Israel:

> For the sons of Israel will remain for many days without king or prince, without sacrifice or sacred pillar and without ephod or household idols. Afterward the sons of Israel will return and seek the Lord their God and David their king; and they will come trembling to the Lord and to His goodness in the last days.

Verse 4 emphasizes Israel's exile as they go "many days without king or prince" and without the temple. But then verse 5 says after this Israel will repent, seek God and the Davidic King, and experience the King's "goodness in the last days."

Next, Hosea 11:9–11 predicts a coming exodus for Israel from exile that results with Israel being reestablished in their land again:

> "I will not execute My fierce anger;
> I will not destroy Ephraim again.

For I am God and not man, the Holy One in your midst,
And I will not come in wrath.
They will walk after the Lord,
He will roar like a lion;
Indeed He will roar
And His sons will come trembling from the west.
They will come trembling like birds from Egypt
And like doves from the land of Assyria;
And I will settle them in their houses," declares the Lord.

So even before Hosea 11:1 is considered we know that Hosea's argument involves an explicit messianic hope in which the Messiah will be part of a second exodus for Israel after a time in which Israel was in exile.

Now consider Hosea 11:1, the verse that later would be quoted in Matthew 2:15:

When Israel was a youth I loved him,
And out of Egypt I called My son.

As most have noted, this is a reference to Israel's historical exodus from Egypt under Moses. The book of Exodus highlights Israel as God's son who is called out of Egypt. As Exodus 4:22–23a states: "Then you shall say to Pharaoh, 'Thus says the Lord, "Israel is My son, My firstborn. So I said to you, 'Let My son go that he may serve Me.'"

It is undeniable that Hosea 11:1 refers to Israel's historical exodus from Egypt under Moses. Yet God's love for Israel in Hosea 11:1 is also evident here and is a key part of Hosea's reasoning. When Israel was young God loved Israel and called Israel "My son." This is tender affection. Hosea 11:2–4 further describes God's love for Israel. God took Israel in His arms and taught Israel how to walk (11:3). So we must note that Hosea 11:1 is not just a history book fact that God caused Israel's exodus from Egypt. It also emphasizes God's love for Israel, which will be prominent in the rest of Hosea 11, including the promise of a future exodus. Israel's first exodus was evidence of God's love and so too will the coming exodus be an act of God's love for Israel.

Sadly, though, Israel disobeyed God by committing idolatry as Hosea 11:2 notes:

> They kept sacrificing to the Baals
> And burning incense to idols.

As a result, Israel will experience captivity by Assyria as Hosea 11:5 states:

> They will not return to the land of Egypt;
> But Assyria—he will be their king
> Because they refused to return to Me.

Exile must occur because of disobedience. Verses 6–7 then describe the terrible consequences this captivity will bring. But verse 8 tells how God's love for Israel will not allow Israel to wallow in suffering and captivity forever:

> "How can I give you up, O Ephraim?
> How can I surrender you, O Israel?
> How can I make you like Admah?
> How can I treat you like Zeboiim?
> My heart is turned over within Me,
> All My compassions are kindled."

Again, note God's love for Israel. "My heart is turned over within Me" and "All My compassions are kindled." Then comes the incredible statement that God will bring a second exodus for Israel with Hosea 11:9–11:

> "I will not execute My fierce anger;
> I will not destroy Ephraim again.
> For I am God and not man, the Holy One in your midst,
> And I will not come in wrath.
> They will walk after the Lord,
> He will roar like a lion;
> Indeed He will roar
> And His sons will come trembling from the west.
> They will come trembling like birds from Egypt
> And like doves from the land of Assyria;
> And I will settle them in their houses," declares the Lord.

Hosea 11:9–11 predicted a coming second exodus for Israel because God loves Israel and Israel is God's son.

We now can evaluate Hosea's authorial logic. Hosea's historical reference to the first exodus in 11:1 does not occur in a vacuum. *Hosea did not mention Israel's first exodus as a history-book fact. He did it to emphasize God's love for Israel. Just as God loved Israel and rescued Israel with an exodus from Egypt under Moses, so, too, He will save and restore Israel with a second exodus under the Davidic King (i.e. Messiah) because of His love.*

When Matthew quotes Hosea 11:1 this is the logic Matthew draws upon. Hosea 11:1 comes with a logic and reasoning from Hosea and Matthew notes this. Matthew quotes Hosea 11:1 to highlight that Jesus is the promised Davidic King who will bring the second exodus that Hosea and other Old Testament prophets predicted. The Messianic hope for exodus in Hosea now meets the arrival of Jesus the Messiah. With Matthew 2:15, Matthew draws a correspondence between Israel's first exodus as God's beloved son, and Israel's coming second exodus through the Messiah as God's beloved Son.

Now we can answer the question, "Is Hosea 11:1 forward looking to Jesus?" If we look at Hosea 11:1 apart from its context the answer appears to be, No. But since Hosea 11:1 is part of a broader argument that God will use the Messiah to lead Israel in a second exodus from captivity, the answer is, Yes! If Hosea predicted a Davidic King to restore Israel (see Hosea 3:4–5), and God's love for Israel is reason for a second exodus (see Hosea 11:9–11), then why wouldn't Hosea 11:1 have a forward-looking aspect to it? The key is to note God's love for Israel at the first exodus as the reason why there will be a second exodus in the future. Israel is God's son and God loves Israel. Jesus is God's Son and He loves Jesus. And God will use Jesus to accomplish an exodus for the nation. The corporate Head of Israel will save the nation. Jesus' experience as God's Son being called out of Egypt fills up or fulfills Israel's experience as God's son being called out of Egypt, and Jesus will be the One who restores Israel from exile.

In sum, when Hosea refers to the previous exodus of Israel from Egypt as God's son in Hosea 11:1, he emphasizes God's love for Israel and that God will once again deliver Israel with another exodus. When Matthew 2:15 refers to Hosea 11:1 these are things Matthew draws upon in a contextual manner, and the fulfillment Jesus will bring for Israel is just what Hosea predicted.

Numbers 23 and 24

Before ending this section, we also want to mention one more contextual factor concerning Israel and Israel's king being linked with the exodus from Egypt theme. This connection between

Israel and Israel's king both coming out of Egypt is seen with the following prophetic oracles of Balaam in Numbers 23 and 24:

> "God brings them [Israel] out of Egypt, He is for them like the horns of the wild ox" (Num. 23:22).

> "God brings him [Israel's King] out of Egypt, He is for him like the horns of the wild ox" (Num. 24:8).

Here both Israel and Israel's King are said to be brought out of Egypt to show a connection between Israel and Israel's King. So before Hosea wrote Hosea 11:1 and Matthew wrote Matthew 2:14–15, Numbers 23:22 and 24:8 connected Israel coming out of Egypt with Israel's King coming out of Egypt.

These texts in Numbers add another dimension to the discussion. Since Hosea knew the Old Testament well, he most probably was aware of this connection. One could say Hosea's theology was in line with what Moses wrote centuries earlier. Who links Israel and Israel's King with coming out of Egypt? Moses, Hosea, and Matthew.

Matthew 2:17–19 / Jeremiah 31:15

Another example of correspondence/fulfillment between Israel and Jesus in the context of messianic hope occurs in Matthew 2:17–19 and its use of Jeremiah 31:15. Jeremiah 31:15 refers to the Babylonian Captivity and the women of Israel weeping bitterly as their young men were taken captive to Babylon via the town of Ramah:

> Thus says the Lord,
> "A voice is heard in Ramah,
> Lamentation and bitter weeping.

Rachel is weeping for her children;

She refuses to be comforted for her children,

Because they are no more."

Jeremiah 31:15 mentions a negative event in Israel's history—the Babylonian Captivity of 586 B.C. This calamity also came to symbolize the mourning and grief Israel has experienced throughout history. As Abner Chou notes, "Jeremiah 31:15 uses Israel's past deportation to describe the entire era of exile."[19] In addition, "Rachel" is a symbol of maternal grief for Israel's sufferings going forward.

Notably, though, the verses immediately after Jeremiah 31:15 foretell restoration for Israel back to its territorial land:

Thus says the Lord,

"Restrain your voice from weeping

And your eyes from tears;

For your work will be rewarded," declares the Lord,

"And they will return from the land of the enemy.

"There is hope for your future," declares the Lord,

"And your children will return to their own territory"

(Jer. 31:16–17).

Put together, exile and tragedy later transition to national restoration.

Jeremiah 31, as a whole, predicted restoration for Israel linked with the New Covenant of verses 31–34. This chapter comes in the middle of Jeremiah 30–33, often known as the Book of Consolation, a hopeful section describing the restoration of

---

19   Abner Chou, *The Hermeneutics of the Biblical Writers: Learning to Interpret Scripture from the Prophets and Apostles* (Grand Rapids: Kregel, 2018), 137.

national Israel after a time of great distress. These chapters foretell Israel's blessing when all the covenants of promise come to
fruition—the Abrahamic, Davidic, and New covenants.

Immediately after Jeremiah 31:15, Rachel is told to stop
weeping because of the coming New Covenant:

> Thus says the Lord,
> "Restrain your voice from weeping
> And your eyes from tears;
> For your work will be rewarded," declares the Lord,
> "And they will return from the land of the enemy.
> "There is hope for your future," declares the Lord,
> "And your children will return to their own territory"
> (Jer. 31:16–17).

Thus, the mention of Rachel weeping in 31:15 cannot be divorced
from the immediate context in which God will remove the cause
of weeping in Israel. Captivity will be followed by restoration.
Hope follows tragedy.

Also, at the center of this restoration for Israel is the ultimate Davidic King—the Messiah—who we now know as Jesus.
Note the messianic hope expectations from Jeremiah 30–33:

Jeremiah 30:8–9:

> "It shall come about on that day," declares the Lord of hosts,
> "that I will break his yoke from off their neck and will tear
> off their bonds; and strangers will no longer make them
> their slaves. But they shall serve the Lord their God and
> David their king, whom I will raise up for them" (empha-
> ses added).

Jeremiah 33:14–16:

"Behold, days are coming," declares the Lord, "when I will fulfill the good word which I have spoken concerning the house of Israel and the house of Judah. In those days and at that time I will cause <u>a righteous Branch of David</u> to spring forth; and He shall execute justice and righteousness on the earth. In those days Judah will be saved and Jerusalem will dwell in safety; and this is the name by which she will be called: the Lord is our righteousness" (emphases added).

Jesus is "David their king" and the "righteous Branch of David" who will bring Israel blessings. So essential for understanding Jeremiah 30–33 and Matthew's use of Jeremiah 31:15 is the messianic hope inherent in this section. The Messiah will turn tragedy into blessings for Israel. Jeremiah 31:15 is a negative verse about a tragic event, but this tragedy is in the context of great hope for Israel, centered in what the Messiah will do.

Matthew's Use of Jeremiah 31:15

Centuries later, Matthew quoted Jeremiah 31:15 concerning the tragedy of infant males slaughtered by Herod at the time of Jesus' advent, and the deep mourning that followed:

Then what had been spoken through Jeremiah the prophet
    was fulfilled:
"A voice was heard in Ramah,
Weeping and great mourning,
Rachel weeping for her children;
And she refused to be comforted,
Because they were no more" (Matt. 2:17–18).

This quotation of Jeremiah 31:15 by Matthew has caused much discussion and debate. How can the deportation of young men to Babylon via Ramah in the sixth-century B.C. relate to Herod's slaughter of infants in Bethlehem in Jesus' day? Doesn't Matthew know Jeremiah 31:15 refers to a historical event and is not a prophecy about Jesus? Isn't young men being taken alive to Babylon different from infant males being slaughtered? Does Matthew not know that Ramah is not Bethlehem? Is Matthew taking Jeremiah 31:15 out of context and thus transforming what fulfillment in Jesus means? To understand what Matthew is doing we must understand the context of Jeremiah 31:15 as discussed above.

Matthew presents Jesus as the Messiah, the Son of David (see Matt. 1:1), who will save Israel (see Matt. 1:21). As was the case with Hosea 11:1, Matthew highlights a correspondence between an important event in Israel's history and an important event in Jesus' life to connect Jesus with Israel and show Jesus is the One who can bring an end to Israel's sufferings. The killing of infants under Herod, as Matthew 2:17–19 describes, continues and "fills up" the mourning that commenced with the Babylonian Captivity. And Jesus is the One who "fills up" and brings the messianic hope of Jeremiah 31 and 30–33 as a whole.

Jesus is the One who brings salvation and restoration. Herod brought a tragic event to Israel, just as the Babylonian Captivity brought tragedy to Israel earlier. But Jesus is the Davidic King of Jeremiah 30–33 who brings salvation and deliverance to Israel.

While exile and suffering have been part of Israel's history, salvation and restoration is also a part of Israel's coming history. Matthew 2:17–19 reveals that Jesus is the end of Israel's story of suffering—the One who transforms Israel's deepest tragedies into ultimate deliverance. Rachel's weeping over the Bethlehem infants is linked with Jesus' birth that marks the beginning of the end of Israel's sorrow. The tragedy of the infants' deaths is not the final word; the Messiah has come to overcome Israel's suffering and ultimately bring deliverance.

In sum, in quoting Jeremiah 31:15, Matthew connects Jesus to Israel's suffering and he also signals that Jesus is the culmination of Israel's hope—the One who transforms mourning into joy, death into life, and exile into restoration.

Summary

Matthew 2:15 / Hosea 11:1 and Matthew 2:17–19 / Jeremiah 31:15 both present Jesus as the fulfillment of Israel's hope. Jesus is the One who will lead Israel in a second exodus (Matt. 2:15) and end Israel's history of tragedies (Matt. 2:17–19). In both texts, events in Israel's history correspond with events in Jesus' life. A messianic hope also exists in the two passages Matthew quotes. This shows the reader that Jesus is the representative Head of Israel who can save and restore the nation.

Significantly, this fulfillment in Jesus is not mystical. Jesus does not absorb or transform the concept of Israel. Instead, Jesus is the One who can lead Israel from suffering and tragedy to hope and a permanent second exodus.

CHAPTER SEVEN

JESUS AS THE ULTIMATE DAVIDIC KING

We noted earlier that one major role Jesus fulfills is that of the ultimate Davidic King who will rule from David's throne in Jerusalem over Israel and all the nations on earth. But one thing that surprised us in our study is how often events in David's life are said to be fulfilled in the life of Jesus. On several occasions things that happen to David correspond to happenings in Jesus' life. These patterns highlight that Jesus is the ultimate son of David and Messiah.

We also noticed that most of these connections involve suffering. While David was God's anointed king, he suffered greatly. So too does Jesus. David's trials and sufferings are said to be filled up or fulfilled in Jesus, the greater David, to show the strong connection between the two in God's plans.

John 13:18 / Psalm 41:9

In John 13, Jesus washed the feet of His disciples just hours before His death. With verse 18 Jesus predicted His betrayal by Judas by quoting a psalm of David:

> I do not speak of all of you. I know the ones I have chosen; but it is that the Scripture may be fulfilled, "He who eats My bread has lifted up his heel against Me."

Jesus viewed His impending betrayal by Judas as fulfillment of Psalm 41:9 and its statement that one eating bread will be a betrayer. Psalm 41 was written by David as a complaint concerning his enemies. In Psalm 41:5 David said, "My enemies speak evil against me." Then with 41:9 David noted that his enemy was a close friend with whom he ate bread:

> Even my close friend in whom I trusted,
> Who ate my bread,
> Has lifted up his heel against me.

This enemy who betrayed David probably is Ahithophel (see 2 Samuel 16–17). Thus, a betrayer in David's life prefigures a betrayer in Jesus' life, the One who is the greater David. So, the one who betrayed David corresponds to Jesus' betrayer—Judas. As S. Lewis Johnson observes, "It is perfectly natural and justifiable to see" David's enemies "as prefiguring the Messiah's enemies."[20]

John 15:25 / Psalm 69:4

With Psalm 69:4 David stated: "Those who hate me without a cause are more than the hairs of my head." Here David declared that his enemies hate him without a good reason. But with John 15:18–25, Jesus connects hatred towards Him with the hatred David experienced. Jesus quoted Psalm 69:4 to say what David experienced was fulfilled with Him: "But they have done this to fulfill the word that is written in their Law, 'THEY HATED ME WITHOUT A CAUSE.'"

---

20 S. Lewis Johnson, *The Old Testament in the New: An Argument for Biblical Inspiration* (Grand Rapids: Zondervan, 1980), 77.

What does this mean? Psalm 69 described David's experiences as a righteous sufferer on God's behalf. Likewise, Jesus, the ultimate Davidic King, is a righteous Sufferer on God's behalf. There is a correspondence between the experiences of David and those of the Son of David—Jesus. The opposition David experienced is "filled up" with the opposition Jesus experienced.

John 19:24 / Psalm 22:18

John 19 describes Jesus' crucifixion. While on the cross the Roman soldiers divided Jesus' outer garments into four parts (v. 23). But when they came to Jesus' seamless tunic they were reluctant to tear it. Verse 24 describes what followed:

> So they said to one another, "Let us not tear it, but cast lots for it, to decide whose it shall be"; this was to fulfill the Scripture: "THEY DIVIDED MY OUTER GARMENTS AMONG THEM, AND FOR MY CLOTHING THEY CAST LOTS."

The dividing of Jesus' garments and the casting of lots for Jesus' tunic was linked with Psalm 22:18 which states, "They divide my garments among them, and for my clothing they cast lots."

It is difficult to know how much of Psalm 22 is describing David's actual experiences and how much is predictive of Jesus' experiences on the cross. Psalm 22:11–18 could be predictive concerning Jesus. Yet, there is a close connection between David as a righteous sufferer for God and Jesus being the ultimate Righteous Sufferer. In sum, with Psalm 22:18, the suffering of David prefigures the suffering of the Messiah. But there also could be an element of explicit messianic prediction since Jesus, not David, literally experienced the conditions of Psalm 22:11–18. As Walter Kaiser notes, "While to a lesser degree it is possible to speak of some of these things happening in the life of David, it is only with that climactic descendant of his, the Messiah, that it is possible to see most of these things fulfilled in detail."[21]

John 19:36 / Psalm 34:20

With Psalm 34:19–20 David celebrated the Lord as a deliverer:

> Many are the afflictions of the righteous,
> But the LORD delivers him out of them all.
> He keeps all his bones,
> Not one of them is broken.

With John 19:36, John applied Psalm 34:20 to the soldiers piercing Jesus' side instead of breaking Jesus' legs:

> For these things came to pass to fulfill the Scripture, "NOT A BONE OF HIM SHALL BE BROKEN."

For John, the words of David were fulfilled with Jesus' bones not being broken while on the cross. A theological truth stated by David is applied to Jesus who is the ultimate example of righteousness.

Luke 23:46 / Psalm 31:5

Psalm 31 describes David's trust in God while in distress. It is the Lord in whom David takes refuge; and it is the Lord who is David's rock and fortress (Ps. 31:1–3). With verse 5 David

---

21   Walter C. Kaiser, Jr., *The Messiah in the Old Testament* (Grand Rapids: Zondervan, 1995), 118.

declared: "Into Your hand I commit my spirit; You have ransomed me, O LORD, God of truth." David trusted the Lord with his life.

Centuries later, while on the cross, Jesus the Messiah quoted David's words of trust in Psalm 31:5:

> And Jesus, crying out with a loud voice, said, "Father, INTO YOUR HANDS I COMMIT MY SPIRIT." Having said this, He breathed His last (Luke 23:46).

The first David trusted God during troubling times, and now the ultimate David, Jesus, trusts His life to God during His darkest moment on the cross. Pao and Schnabel point out that Jesus' quotation of Psalm 31:5 reveals two truths. First, it demonstrates that Jesus' death fulfills God's purposes in the midst of darkness. And second, it reveals "that he [God] will rescue him [Jesus] from his enemies and raise him from the dead."[22] Trust in God was true for both David and the Son of David—Jesus.

---

22 David W. Pao and Eckhard J. Schnabel, "Luke," in *Commentary on the New Testament Use of the Old Testament*, eds. G. K. Beale and D. A. Carson (Grand Rapids: Baker, 2007), 399.

CHAPTER EIGHT

JESUS AS THE SUBSTANCE OF MOSAIC COVENANT CEREMONIES AND FEASTS

B iblical covenants are a major part of the Bible's storyline. In fact, much of the Scripture's narrative can be understood by tracing the unfolding of the biblical covenants in history. The Mosaic Covenant played a major role in God's plans. This covenant functioned as Israel's constitution and means for living and pleasing God from Exodus 19 until the death of Jesus on the cross (see Eph. 2:15). If obeyed, it was also the means for Israel remaining in the land of promise, stemming from the Abrahamic Covenant. Israel, of course, did not obey and thus the need for a new and better covenant arose. One of the major things Jesus does is transition His people from the era of the Mosaic Covenant to the era of the New Covenant. As Romans 10:4 states, "For Christ is the end of the law for righteousness to everyone who believes."

This transition from the Mosaic Covenant to the New Covenant was predicted in Jeremiah 31:31–32:

> "Behold, days are coming," declares the Lord, "when I will make a new covenant with the house of Israel and with the house of Judah, not like the covenant which I made with their fathers in the day I took them by the hand to bring them out of the land of Egypt, My covenant which they broke, although I was a husband to them," declares the Lord.

Since the section in which this statement appears, Jeremiah 30–33, contains a messianic hope (see Jer. 30:8–9; 33:14–16), it highlights a strong connection between the coming New Covenant, which would replace the Mosaic Covenant, and the ultimate Davidic King—the Messiah. It takes the Messiah to bring the New Covenant. John the Baptist referred to this fact when he said of Jesus, "He will baptize you with the Holy Spirit and fire" (Matt. 3:11b). Jesus the Messiah will baptize His followers with the New Covenant ministry of the Holy Spirit and will bring judgment to those who oppose Him.

Jesus anticipated the transition to the New Covenant His death would accomplish at the Last Supper when He declared, "This cup which is poured out for you is the new covenant in My blood" (Luke 22:20b).

In sum, Jesus is the Messiah who transitions His people from the Mosaic Covenant to the New Covenant with a better priesthood and sacrifice.

Jesus and the Feasts of Israel

Leviticus 23 outlines seven key feasts or holidays for Israel, which are part of the Mosaic Covenant: (1) Passover; (2) Unleavened Bread; (3) First fruits; (4) Weeks; (5) Trumpets; (6) Day of Atonement; and (7) Tabernacles. These are tied to Israel's agricultural seasons. The first four relate to the Spring calendar and the last three to the Fall.

Not only were these feasts holidays for the Israelite people, but their significances also pointed towards Jesus. As Howard and Rosenthal point out:

> These seven feasts typify the sequence, timing, and significance of the major events of the Lord's redemptive career.

> They commence at Calvary where Jesus voluntarily gave
> Himself for the sins of the world (Passover), and climax
> at the establishment of the messianic Kingdom at the
> Messiah's second coming (Tabernacles).[23]

The first four feasts particularly relate to Jesus' first coming, while the last three have special significance for Jesus' second advent.

Concerning the ceremonies and feasts of the Mosaic Covenant Paul said, "the substance belongs to Christ" (Col. 2:16–17). The term for "substance" can be translated "body" and indicates that Jesus embodies the essence of what the ceremonies and feasts of the Mosaic Covenant represented.

Passover

The first Passover in Exodus 12 commemorates Israel's deliverance from Egypt through the lamb's blood. It was to be celebrated every year. Jesus is the ultimate Lamb of God who takes away the sins of the world (see John 1:29). Paul explicitly connected the Passover and Jesus when he declared, "Christ our Passover also has been sacrificed" (1 Cor. 5:7).

First Fruits

The Feast of First Fruits, explained in Leviticus 23:9–14, was a Jewish celebration marking the offering of the first barley sheaf to God. First Fruits occurred on the day after the Sabbath following Passover, pointing to the hope for a bountiful future harvest. With 1 Corinthians 15:20–23, Paul links the Feast of

---

23   Kevin Howard and Marvin Rosenthal, *The Feasts of the Lord: God's Prophetic Calendar from Calvary to the Kingdom* (Thomas Nelson), 14.

First Fruits with Jesus' resurrection and what this means for the coming resurrection of those in union with Jesus: "Christ is the first fruits of those who are asleep" (1 Cor. 15:20). Then Paul mentions Christ as the "first fruits," or first-step of a three-stage resurrection program (see 1 Cor. 15:23–24). Jesus' resurrection, occurring during the Feast of First Fruits, connects Him to this celebration and secures the hope of eternal life for Christians.

Weeks (Pentecost)

The Feast of Weeks occurs seven weeks (50 days) after Passover. It was primarily a harvest festival celebrating the end of the grain harvest and the offering of the first fruits to God. It was on the Day of Pentecost, in Acts 2, that Jesus poured forth the New Covenant ministry of the Holy Spirit upon His followers in Jerusalem which launched a great harvest of Jesus followers that occurs throughout this present age.

Day of Atonement

Leviticus 16 is the primary passage that details the Day of Atonement, explaining the responsibilities of the high priest and the significance of the day for the people of Israel. Hebrews 9:11–14 shows how Jesus' New Covenant priesthood and sacrifice transcend the Day of Atonement under the Mosaic Covenant. With the Day of Atonement under the Mosaic Covenant, the high priest entered the Most Holy Place to make sacrifices for sin, but the efficacy of these were only temporary and could not cleanse the conscience. But Jesus, the true High Priest, entered the heavenly sanctuary and offered His own blood, securing eternal redemption and internal transformation for all who believe.

The feasts of Israel had great historical significance and were to be kept by Israel under the Mosaic Covenant era. They also point to Jesus who is the embodiment of the main messages of the feasts. They reveal truths that relate to Jesus, both with His first coming and for His second advent. Yet, we must also understand that the feasts of Israel are no longer binding to be kept in this present age. According to Paul, in Colossians 2:16–17, ceremonial activities under the Mosaic Covenant are no longer binding for observance because of Jesus:

> Therefore no one is to act as your judge in regard to food or drink or in respect to a festival or a new moon or a Sabbath day—things which are a mere shadow of what is to come; but the substance belongs to Christ.

Paul's statement that the ceremonies and feasts are "a mere shadow of what is to come" underscores the transition from the Mosaic Covenant to the New Covenant in Christ.

Under the Mosaic Covenant era before Jesus, ceremonial activities concerning food and drink, festivals, new moon, and the Sabbath were requirements for Israel to keep. But with Jesus and the New Covenant era those activities are no longer binding for God's people. The food laws of the Mosaic Covenant were abrogated when Jesus "declared all foods clean" according to Mark 7:19 (cf. Acts 10:10–16).

Paul likens these Mosaic requirements to a "shadow," (*skia*) that gives way to something greater. This something greater is Jesus who is the "substance" of those things. The Greek term Paul uses here is *soma*, which can be translated as "body," "reality," or "substance." Jesus embodies what the feasts represented.

Thus, the Mosaic Covenant and its elements are called "shadow" by Paul. Hebrews 10:1 also stated that the "Law . . . has only a shadow of the good things to come." In this context the "Law" is the Mosaic Covenant/Law, and the good things to come refer to Jesus and His New Covenant. Thus, the reality of Jesus means observance of Mosaic Covenant ceremonies no longer is required in the New Covenant era.

This reality does not mean that Israel's feasts lose all historical significance or cannot be celebrated in any way. For example, Paul stated in 1 Corinthians 5:7 that "Christ our Passover also has been sacrificed." So Christ is the ultimate Passover sacrifice. But in Luke 22:14–16 Jesus stated that in the future kingdom of God He will once again eat the Passover meal with His disciples:

> When the hour had come, He reclined at the table, and the apostles with Him. And He said to them, "I have earnestly desired to eat this Passover with you before I suffer; for I say to you, I shall never again eat it until it is fulfilled in the kingdom of God."

When the kingdom of God arrives we will eat a Passover meal with Jesus as we celebrate Him being the ultimate meaning of the Passover.

Zechariah 14:16 also reveals that nations will commemorate the Feast of Booths in Jesus' coming earthly kingdom:

> Then it will come about that any who are left of all the nations that went against Jerusalem will go up from year to year to worship the King, the Lord of hosts, and to celebrate the Feast of Booths.

The Proper Significance of
Colossians 2:16–17 and Hebrews 7–10

At this point we address a misunderstanding that sometimes occurs with Colossians 2:16–17 and Hebrews 7–10. What these two sections specifically address is Jesus' relationship to the Mosaic Covenant/Law and its ceremonies and feasts. They indicate a transition from the era of the Mosaic Covenant to the New Covenant era and all this entails. The fact that the Mosaic Law is a "shadow" of the New Covenant, and Israel's ceremonies and feasts are a "shadow" of Jesus, does not mean that everything in the Old Testament is a shadow. We note this because often people will lump statements about the Mosaic Covenant with the entire Old Testament. A statement that the Mosaic Covenant and its elements are shadows does not mean the entire Old Testament is a shadow.

The Mosaic Covenant was a temporary conditional covenant that Israel broke. Thus, the New Covenant would replace it (see Jer. 31:31–32). While mandated to keep the Mosaic Covenant, this covenant did not enable sinful Israelites to keep it. But the New Covenant brings enablement through the indwelling Holy Spirit and a new heart, things that were not part of the Mosaic Covenant.

However, the covenants of promise—Abrahamic, Davidic, and New—are different in nature from the Mosaic Covenant. They are unconditional and eternal covenants. The parties and promises of these covenants are not temporary shadows. This includes the importance of earth, Israel, Israel's land, physical blessings, geo-political nations, Jerusalem, the throne of David, etc.

Colossians 2:16–17 and Hebrews 7–10 are not evidence that the parties and elements of the covenants of promise are shadows that pass away or are transformed spiritually in Christ. They are not saying that all the matters mentioned in the paragraph above have been spiritually transformed. We must not take statements about Mosaic Covenant realities being a shadow and then impose the "shadow" concept on the covenants of promise and their elements. This leads to serious error.

CHAPTER NINE

JESUS AND THE GUARANTEE OF PROPHECIES NOT YET FULFILLED

A s we have seen, Jesus fulfills and accomplishes the Old Testament in various ways. Yet since there are two comings of Jesus, there are Old Testament predictions and expectations that await future fulfillment with Jesus' return to earth. On several occasions Jesus himself referred to Old Testament prophecies that still needed to happen after His first advent. Below we note several of these.

Saints Shining in the Kingdom

In Matthew 13:41–43, with His Parable of the Wheat and the Tares, Jesus predicted that His followers (the wheat) would coexist with the devil's people (the tares) until Jesus returned with His angels to separate them. He quoted Daniel 12:3 about God's people shining in the kingdom after His return to make this point:

> The Son of Man will send forth His angels, and they will gather out of His kingdom all stumbling blocks, and those who commit lawlessness, and will throw them into the furnace of fire; in that place there will be weeping and gnashing of teeth. Then THE RIGHTEOUS WILL

SHINE FORTH AS THE SUN in the kingdom of their
Father (Matt. 13:41–43a).

Thus, Jesus placed the fulfillment of Daniel 12:3 and its prediction of the righteous people shining in the kingdom of God after a
time of tribulation in the future with His second advent to earth.

The Coming Elijah

With the last two verses of the Old Testament, Malachi predicted
the coming of Elijah in connection with the Day of the Lord and
the restoring of all things:

> "Behold, I am going to send you Elijah the prophet before
> the coming of the great and terrible day of the Lord. He
> will restore the hearts of the fathers to their children and
> the hearts of the children to their fathers, so that I will not
> come and smite the land with a curse" (Malachi 4:5–6).

Fast forward to Jesus' time. While noting the great significance of John the Baptist's historical role, Jesus looked forward to
a coming Elijah figure who would be part of the coming restoration of all things:

> And His [Jesus'] disciples asked Him, "Why then do the
> scribes say that Elijah must come first?" And He answered
> and said, "Elijah is coming and will restore all things" (Matt.
> 17:10–11).

This shows that Jesus expected a coming person to
completely fulfill the prediction of Elijah arriving in connection
with the Day of the Lord according to Malachi 4:5–6.

The AD 70 Destruction of Jerusalem

Daniel 9:26a predicted that Jerusalem and the temple (i.e. sanctuary) would be destroyed after the cutting off of the Messiah:

> Then after the sixty-two weeks the Messiah will be cut off and have nothing, and the people of the prince who is to come will destroy the city and the sanctuary.

With Luke 21:20–24 Jesus predicted the coming destruction of Jerusalem and the temple by the Roman armies that would occur in AD 70 in fulfillment of Daniel 9:26:

> "But when you see Jerusalem surrounded by armies, then recognize that her desolation is near.... because these are days of vengeance, so that all things which are written will be fulfilled."

When Jesus offered these words the destruction of Jerusalem and the temple were about thirty-seven years away. This is another example of Jesus expecting the coming fulfillment of a predicted event in the Old Testament after His first coming.

The Abomination of Desolation

With His Olivet Discourse Jesus predicted a coming Abomination of Desolation in line with Daniel 9:27 that would impact Jerusalem and the temple by the coming Antichrist:

> "Therefore when you see the abomination of desolation which was spoken of through Daniel the prophet, standing in the holy place (let the reader understand)" (Matt. 24:15).

This Abomination of Desolation is still future from our point in history, but Matthew 24:15 shows again that Jesus expected literal fulfillment of an event that was still future from His current standpoint in the first century.

Worst Tribulation in History

Daniel 12:1b foretold a coming time period that would be the worst in history:

> And there will be a time of distress such as never occurred since there was a nation until that time; and at that time your people, everyone who is found written in the book, will be rescued.

Relying on the truth of Daniel 12:1, Jesus predicted a "great tribulation" that would be the worst time in human history:

> "For then there will be a great tribulation, such as has not occurred since the beginning of the world until now, nor ever will" (Matt. 24:21).

Cosmic Signs

Jesus also foretold cosmic signs in fulfillment of Isaiah 13:10 and Joel 2:31:

> "But immediately after the tribulation of those days the sun will be darkened, and the moon will not give its light, and the stars will fall from the sky, and the powers of the heavens will be shaken" (Matt. 24:29).

The coming cosmic signs involving sun, moon, and stars will be a fulfillment of various Old Testament prophecies.

Son of Man Coming on Clouds

Daniel 7:13–14 details how the Son of Man (Messiah) comes on the clouds of heaven before God to receive all authority. Zechariah 12:10 foretells Israel's repentance and salvation during a time of distress. With Matthew 24:30, Jesus relied upon the prophecies of Daniel 7:13–14 and Zechariah 12:10 when discussing His return to earth:

> And then the sign of the Son of Man will appear in the sky, and then all the tribes of the earth will mourn, and they will see the Son of Man coming on the clouds of the sky with power and great glory (Matt. 24:30).

Thus, at the time of the Olivet Discourse Jesus viewed the fulfillment of Daniel 7:13–14 and Zechariah 12:10 as still needing to occur. This will happen with Jesus' second coming.

Gathering of Israel with a Trumpet

Isaiah 27:12–13 predicted a coming regathering of Israel after Tribulation in connection with a trumpet blast:

> In that day the Lord will start His threshing from the flowing stream of the Euphrates to the brook of Egypt, and you will be gathered up one by one, O sons of Israel. It will come about also in that day that a great trumpet will be blown, and those who were perishing in the land of Assyria and who were scattered in the land of Egypt will come

and worship the Lord in the holy mountain at Jerusalem
(emphases added).

Jesus says this will occur after the Tribulation that is
described in Matthew 24:31:

And He will send forth His angels with a great trumpet
and they will gather together His elect from the four winds,
from one end of the sky to the other.

Messiah to Rule the Nations

Psalm 2:8–9 stated that God's Son, the Messiah, will be given
the nations as His inheritance and He will rule the nations
with a rod of iron. This still awaits future fulfillment. In the
90s AD, Jesus quoted Psalm 2:8–9 in Revelation 2:26–27 when
discussing how He will share His reign over the nations with
the church:

He who overcomes, and he who keeps My deeds until the
end, to him <u>I will give authority over the nations; and he
shall rule them with a rod of iron</u>, as the vessels of the potter
are broken to pieces, as I also have received authority from
My Father (emphases added).

Revelation 19:15a also places Jesus' kingdom reign over the
nations at the time of His second coming: "From His mouth
comes a sharp sword, so that with it He may strike down the
nations, and He will rule them with a rod of iron."

Even in the 90s AD, Jesus expected a future fulfillment of
Psalm 2 in which He will reign over the nations with a rod of
iron. He will share that reign with His followers.

More examples could be given. Jesus is the One who unleashes the Day of the Lord (see Rev. 6:1), and He is the One who will bring about resurrections, judgments, and the kingdom of God with His return to earth. But these show that Jesus expected future fulfillment of Old Testament prophecies that were not fulfilled at the time of His first coming.

CHAPTER TEN

CONCLUSION

The issue of how Jesus fulfills the Old Testament is one we should strive to understand accurately. It helps us appreciate even more deeply what God is accomplishing through Jesus.

In this work we strived to offer specific answers to what fulfillment in Jesus actually is—and what it is not. In sum, we argued that Jesus is the means for the accomplishing of all Old Testament prophecies, promises, and covenants in all their details with all the parties to whom these were made. On the contrary, we do not see Jesus transforming, dissolving, or making Old Testament promises vanish. This metaphysical personalism approach is not biblical and takes away from the glories of what Jesus is doing through His two comings to earth.

We also noted that the Bible's storyline is multi-dimensional and complex involving many strategic events, themes, individuals, promises, covenants, prophecies, and more. The ways Jesus fulfills the Old Testament is related to what is actually being fulfilled. Thus, we pointed out six major ways Jesus fulfills the Old Testament:

1. Jesus Accomplishes the Specific Details of Messianic Prophecies
2. Jesus Completes Messianic Hope Expectations
3. Jesus Realizes Israel's Hope of Exodus from Exile (Correspondence + Messianic Hope)

4.   Jesus Culminates Patterns that began with David

5.   Jesus Is the Substance of Mosaic Covenant Ceremonies and Feasts

6.   Jesus Guarantees the Future Fulfillment of Old Testament Prophecies that Have Not Occurred Yet

As we stated earlier this work has not been exhaustive. More could be said on almost every category we have discussed. But hopefully it has challenged the reader to think more deeply on this issue and to ponder, "What does it really mean for Jesus to fulfill the Old Testament?"